D1568917

Treatment of
Abuse and Addiction

Treatment of Abuse and Addiction
A HOLISTIC APPROACH

Arthur P. Ciaramicoli Ed.D., Ph.D

JASON ARONSON INC.
Northvale, New Jersey
London

The author gratefully acknowledges permission to quote material from the following source: *Starving to Death in a Sea of Objects: The Anorexia Nervosa Syndrome*, by John Sours, copyright © 1980 Jason Aronson Inc.

This book was set in 11½ pt. Hiroshige Book by Alpha Graphics of Pittsfield, New Hampshire, and printed and bound by Book-mart Press, Inc. of North Bergen, New Jersey.

Library of Congress Cataloging-in-Publication Data

Ciaramicoli, Arthur P.
    Treatment of abuse and addiction : a
  holistic approach / by Arthur P. Ciaramicoli.
        p. cm.
    Includes bibliographical references and index.
    ISBN 0-7657-0087-5 (alk. paper)
    1. Substance abuse—Treatment. 2. Adult child abuse victims—
  Rehabilitation. 3. Group psychotherapy. 4. Eating disorders—
  Treatment. 5. Self-esteem. 6. Managed mental health care.
  I. Title.
  RA564.C53   1997
  616.85'822390651—dc21   97-11439

Printed in the United States of America on acid-free paper. Jason Aronson Inc. offers books and cassettes. For information and catalog write to Jason Aronson Inc., 230 Livingston Street, Northvale, New Jersey 07647-1731. Or visit our website: http://www.aronson.com

To my wife Karen, the woman with the golden heart,
and our two beautiful daughters, Alaina and Erica

Contents

Acknowledgments

To my wife Karen: your zest for life has always helped me balance mine. Thank you so much for your love, support, and encouragement throughout the writing of this book and throughout our marriage.

To our daughter Alaina: your bright personality, quick wit, and warmth are a wonderful joy to witness every day. Thank you for the motivating notes while I was writing and the constant love you give to your family.

To our daughter Erica: your determination and courage have always been an inspiration to me. Conversations with you enliven my spirit as your curiosity forces me to explain life with clarity. Thank you for your continual enthusiasm about my work.

To my father Arthur, my mother Camie, and my brother David: your lives have not been in vain. Each day I think of each of you in ways that help me to help others.

To my long term friends and family who have supported and loved me throughout my life and especially through the writing of this book: Jeanne and Mark Fitzpatrick, Joanne and Tim Goggins, Valerie Sawyer-Smith and Peter Smith, Gerry and Richard Tessicini, Diane and Richard Werner, and Donna and Philip Wood.

To my colleague and friend Andrea Levy-Wallerstein, LICSW: your belief in the power of human relationships has been most motivating. Thank you for asking the hard questions and waiting until the answers became clear.

To my colleague, running partner, and above all good friend Robert Cherney, PhD.: thank you for your encouragement and faith in my abilities. You are truly a kindred spirit in search of the balanced life. It's also a relief to know someone who is as intense as I am.

To Gurucharan Singh Khalsa, Ph.D.: thank you for reviewing this manuscript. Your ability to simplify complex notions without sacrificing meaning is most appreciated.

To Rhoda Markowitz, head librarian, MetroWest Medical Center: thank you for your assistance and patience. You saved time when it was scarce.

To Judy Deal, typist and editor: thank you for being so gracious, competent, and encouraging.

To Rosanna Mazzei, editorial assistant, at Jason Aronson: thank you for your kindness and patience. You made the choice of a publisher easy. To David Kaplan, copy editor: thank you for the arduous task of reviewing the entire text in detail. Your comments are appreciated. Thank you to the entire Jason Aronson staff for making this process as painless as possible.

To my colleagues in the Department of Behavioral Medicine at MetroWest Medical Center: I have learned so much over the years from your dedication and therapeutic expertise. Health care has become difficult but your hearts remain in the right place.

I am most appreciative to my greatest teachers, the clients who have had the courage to come for help. Always remember that you have given me more than you have taken. The privilege has truly been mine.

Introduction

This project has evolved from observations of many years of clinical practice that clearly indicate the need for greater understanding of those who have suffered abuse, developed subsequent addictions, and are least likely to travel the path toward holistic health.

There is a rising and urgent need to deliver holistic and alternative medicine modalities to the increasing numbers of patients who present themselves to managed care health providers. The goal is to help clients attain self-sustained "fitness"—defined as a comprehensive balance of physical and emotional capacities, integrated to allow healthy interactions with others, a stable sense of the self, and the skill to cope with change and challenge. Fitness defined this way reduces health care cost, enhances the productivity and health of the client, and works toward a conscious self-sustained health effort on the part of the client, with the health care system serving as a partner and advisor.

The key problems to implementing this imperative for a new direction of service are:

1. There are increasing populations of clients who suffer from both abuse and addiction.
2. Most approaches to using programs of alternative medicine erroneously presuppose a stable, fairly developed sense of self in the clients.
3. Clients with histories of both abuse and addiction need a clearly defined interactional process to stabilize their sense of self, improve their reactions to stress and challenge, and increase their ability to comply with the health habits and recommendations that form a core of alternative medicine support.
4. We need a clear treatment provision model that takes the client from the most disrupted state of unstable self, low self-esteem, and irrational beliefs that cause dysfunction to the functional states of motivated, positive self-regard and efficacy. These modes must integrate the specific needs of this population with the organizational needs of the evolving managed care systems, and serve as a filter for the types of alternative treatment appropriate at each stage of the client's rejuvenation to full fitness.

This book addresses the need for those in the field of mental health, and for our society as a whole, to expand and reevaluate our understanding of the development and treatment of injurious behavior toward oneself, abuse of others, and the various addictions that are used to soothe a weakened sense of self. Classical analytic theory, with its emphasis on instinctual drives, has underestimated the interactional origins of abuse (masochism/sadism). This book highlights a group psychotherapy model developed over the last several years that provides intensive opportunities for individuals to develop continuous positive self-regard. This experience has been found to significantly decrease negativity in the face of conflict or in the midst of increased intimacy. The key to successful treatment is the development of a stable sense of self in the client, combined with interactional skills that manage conflict, intimacy, and other interpersonal conditions.

Individuals who have suffered from the dual diagnosis of abuse and addiction do not, and probably cannot, utilize the vast potential of the holistic health movement. Alternative medicine treatment plans often ignore the great number of clients who lack a stable sense of self. With the approach detailed here, we can use alternative medicine with effectiveness and with the advantage of developing "fitness autonomy" in clients, which will lower the cost of long-term care. The goal of this project, which began several years ago, is to develop a group psychotherapy model that clarifies interactional aspects of disturbances and uses interactional elements of healing. This model would facilitate the development of a stable sense of self that is able to tap the enormous potential of the holistic health movement, and to adapt to a rapidly changing world without experiencing anxiety and impulsiveness.

The literature on aggression, sadism, masochism, trauma, group psychotherapy, and holistic health is reviewed and placed in clinical perspective. Chapter 1 discusses abuse of self and others as it pertains to gender differences, but with interactional rather than gender-specific origins emphasized. Chapter 2 describes the advantages of a biopsychosocial model of addiction and recovery, primarily focused on alcoholism, substance abuse, and eating disorders. This comprehensive point of view is parallel to the concept of holism as individuals are seen in their entirety rather than from one narrow perspective or another.

Chapter 3 reviews the group therapy literature, with a particular emphasis on outcome studies, group composition, and therapeutic perspectives. This chapter discusses the value of tailoring group type (psychoeducative, psychodynamic) and leader persuasion (object relations, self psychology, social systems theory) to phase of treatment (early recovery) and diagnosis (affective, personality, psychotic disorders). Major diagnostic groups are reviewed and recommendations for group treatment are made. The section on therapeutic perspectives serves as a guide to an interpersonal group model of healing. The five necessary elements for facilitating positive change—empathy, interactional balance, tension management, internalization, interpretation—and methods of establishing a comprehensive group therapy program, be it inpatient, partial, day treatment, or outpatient, are examined. Selection criteria for various disorders are discussed, and research is reviewed and compared with clinical experience. Individuals are ideally seen as moving from homogeneous, psychoeducational experiences to mixed, interactive psychotherapy groups where diversity and dissimilarity can be dealt with constructively. Group psychotherapy is considered a primary modality, playing a critical role in helping individuals with a range of capabilities cope with and adapt to changes in relationships and in society.

To provide the reader with a sense of the group model advocated, Chapter 4 describes the treatment of five courageous individuals who participated in the therapeutic journey toward holistic health. Detailed accounts are provided of the evolution of their stable sense of self.

Chapter 5 discusses the efficacy of holistic health and the therapeutic pathway that leads to the evolution of a solid sense of self. Individuals learn to let go of unhealthy addictions and behaviors, and they become active rather than passive learners, now filtering information rather than ingesting it unexamined. The individual's newly formed sense of self allows for internal consistency in one's identity and reasonable management of anxiety in the face of change. One learns that through initiative, motivation, and competent self-direction new challenges can be mastered, and new learning can be integrated into an ever-expanding self.

Fitness is an overall state of good health and well-being owing to the ability to care for the body, mind, and spirit as an integrated whole. Fitness, as a comprehensive entity, involves physical ability, emotional balance, and a sense of purpose and meaning in one's life. Chapter 5 reviews recent developments in exercise regimes; nutrition; vitamin, herb, and hormone supplements; alternative medicine; and the role of altruism and spirituality in health.

Chapter 6 discusses managed care as it pertains to quality care, and addresses the need of psychotherapists of all orientations to cope with the rapid changes in health care coverage. Recommendations are made regarding adherence to the medical necessity clause that establishes need for treatment. Criteria for joining particular managed care panels are discussed, and directives are provided for negotiating with insurance companies.

⟪ 1 ⟫

Abuse of Self and Others: Gender Differences and Managed Care Implications

The correlation between being abused, becoming abusive to self or others, and developing subsequent addictions is quite high (Martin et al. 1994, Seppa 1996). To treat this developmental sequence, clinicians must understand the origins of masochism and sadism. Traditional psychoanalysis developed an incomplete model of sadism and masochism. This chapter corrects the most common biases and distortions in that model. In particular, the origins of sadism and masochism, complications of gender, and countertransference issues are examined in detail.

The denial of trauma and severe abuse has historical origins in our culture as well as roots in the history of psychotherapy and psychoanalysis. We have traditionally underestimated the reality and frequency of sexual and physical abuse. The medical community was biased by Freud's analysis of the origins of hysteria and masochism. Freud's early writings on the origins of hysteria reveal his ambivalence regarding the responsibility of perpetrator and victim. In the "Specific Aetiology of Hysteria" (1896) he first states: "The symptoms of hysteria can only be understood if they are traced back to experiences which have a traumatic effect and that these psychical traumas refers to the patient's sexual life" (p. 163). Freud, at this juncture, is clearly indicating that the origin of hysteria is rooted in actual sexual abuse rather than produced by fantasy and wishful longings. He goes on to add, however, "I have found specific determinants of hysteria-sexual passivity during the presexual period in every case of hysteria (including two male cases) which I have analyzed" (p. 163). Freud then adds his most damaging comments as he differentiates male from female in terms of ability to provoke abuse, "A path is laid open to an understanding of why hysteria is far and away more frequent in members of the female sex; for even in childhood they are more liable to provoke sexual attacks" (p. 163). Freud has completed the circle that began with a conceptualization that hysteria is caused by real trauma, to a position of holding the victim accountable for provoking abuse; ultimately this was labeled female masochism.

Judith Herman, in her already classic text *Trauma and Recovery* (1992), ironically indicates that Freud's initial view in *Aetiology of Hysteria* "rivals contemporary clinical descriptions of the effects of childhood sexual abuse. It is a brilliant, compassionate, eloquently argued, closely reasoned document" (p. 13). Herman goes on to indicate that Freud unfortunately never returned to these early formulations again as he moved to a position supporting female seduction and erotic excitement as precipitants in the famous case of Dora.

> The man who had pursued the investigation the farthest and grasped its implications the most completely retreated in later life into the most rigid denial. In the process, he disavowed his female patients. Though he continued to focus on his patients' sexual lives, he no longer acknowledged the exploitative nature of women's real experiences. With a stubborn persistence that drove him into ever greater convolutions of theory. He insisted that women imagined and longed for abusive sexual encounters of which they complained. [p. 19]

Freud, for reasons that were never entirely clear, could not maintain the reality that Herman, Bessel van der Kolk (1987), and other trauma experts have sought to highlight. This painful reality is that adults sexually and physically abuse children, that the origin of hysteria, and, in particular, posttraumatic stress disorder, is not oedipal fantasy but actual trauma induced by parents and other significant authority figures.

The concept of masochism as an expression of intrinsic feminine nature has traumatized female psychotherapy patients and has created a misperception of reality. The view of destructive aggression as an innate instinct and nucleus of drive theory has similarly ill-served male patients. Despite years of efforts to establish biological or genetic origins of violence, the National Research Council concluded in 1993 that there is no unique biological marker that differentiates violent individuals. Nevertheless, this bias of male aggression has prevented exploration of interpersonal and gender role origins and remedies.

This chapter explores the interpersonal origins of abuse and identifies remedies for these disturbances. Freud's initial focus on the interpersonal was later replaced by extreme emphasis on the intrapsychic and instinct-drive theory. Remnants of this point of view still persist today as cultural biases regarding male sadism and female masochism indicate that these character formations are inherent to gender, and thus support the classical analytic position that these behaviors are instinctual and can only be contained through society's regulation of man's destructive nature. This chapter also highlights the retraumatization of victims of abuse by the psychotherapist's implications that they actually sought out abuse. The discussion includes the development of standards of treatment based on instinctual origins of abuse, and standards based on the contemporary understanding of sadism and masochism as by-products of many failed relationships with significant others. Attributing aggression and acts of aggression to either a female masochism fantasy or an innate male nucleus of aggression limits our understanding of the problem of addiction and abuse. We need to focus on the interpersonal and gender cognition origins of these behaviors. Then a model of treatment that is based on learning and skills can be developed.

ORIGINS OF MASOCHISM
AND FEMALE DEVELOPMENT

Masochism has been described as an expression of intrinsic feminine nature. Freud's conceptualization of masochism as erotized aggression led to the perception that masochistic individuals experience pleasure in pain and interactionally utilize this propensity as a weapon, sometimes described as the weapon of the weak (Freud 1919). In fact, clinical experience indicates that the function of masochistic behavior varies from serving as protection from guilt (moral masochism as a defense against sexual anxiety), to maintaining relationships through passivity and submission, to providing self-esteem through identification with a masochistic parent ("I can tolerate any pain just like my mother"), to being intertwined with sadomasochistic excitement functioning as a means of intensely engaging another to mitigate dangers of separating, loss, loneliness, hurt, and destructive guilt (Glick and Meyers 1988).

The one area of agreement in the literature on masochism is that origin and function are multidetermined and represent fixations of different developmental phases, with no particular theory of causality being all encompassing (Ornstein 1991, Sugarman 1991). The Novicks' (1991) review of forty-one cases of masochism does, however, provide needed insight regarding several self-abuse postures that are quite representative. They emphasize the defense of omnipotence as common to all masochistic categories. The caregiver's chronic failure to meet age-appropriate needs results in the child's utilization of this defense as a means of transforming helpless frustration into a sense of being special and immensely significant. Painful experiences are turned into special situations where the child, with the help of his or her self-serving parent, becomes responsible for the distress and discomfort of the adult and thus attains a unique and powerful position infused with magical ideation. Subsequently, the child comes to believe that achievements are also attained magically, which contributes to a lack of patience in the gradual attainment of proficiencies. Individuals tend to hold onto this sense of specialness with tenacity, and this resistance is reminiscent of how often the individual with masochistic character complains of feeling guilty for disappointing others. Guilt is often unconsciously associated with grandiosity as one's actions are seen as extremely important to others, even if in a negative direction. Essentially, the failure of confirming balanced parental interactions forces the child to turn to omnipotence.

Hughes and Wells (1991) further develop origins of masochism from an object relations perspective, with particular emphasis on resultant relational choices with adult partners. They describe a characteristic relationship with parents that is marked not by overt cruelty, but rather by intense ambivalence and subtle hostility. These parents tend to project blame, while being overprotective at other times, making individuation difficult, if not impossible. Attachment and separation are met with mixed feelings that create confusion in the child, who adopts denial as a counteractive defense to parental projection and projective identification.

The authors emphasize that object choices are based on the early paradigm in which children come to believe that they are most loved when suffering. They explain how the choice of the borderline or narcissistic character follows:

> Because of the fluid ego boundaries that these latter personality types tend to manifest, they are ideal candidates for assuming the role of the masochist's partner. Due to their tendencies to merge, borderline and narcissistic individuals are able to penetrate the masochist's rigid defenses and enable them to feel connected. Borderline or narcissistic partners initially fulfill the masochist's underlying wish for symbiosis and later help to recapitulate the erratic environment of the masochist's childhood. Furthermore, narcissistic and borderline individuals have tendencies to

use projection and projection identification (as the masochist's parent did). The menu that the narcissistic or borderline partner "feeds" the masochist thus tastes a lot like "mom's home cooking." [p. 66]

Masochistic thinking and behavior then has functional intrapsychic and interpersonal purpose. Masochism can be conceptualized as a compromised manner of loving due to a deep conviction that pain is the prerequisite for pleasure, or that pain is experienced simultaneously with pleasure. Female patients who provoke and seek out danger are too often viewed as primarily enjoying suffering, rather than as individuals who have adapted to the only method available to engender consistent involvement from abusive caregivers.

Herman (1992) stresses the continued contempt and bias that is still predominant today regarding the origin of female abuse:

Self-blame is congruent with normal forms of thought of early childhood in which the self is taken as the reference point for all events. It is congruent with the thought process of traumatized people of all ages who search for faults in their own behavior in an effort to make sense out of what has happened to them. In an environment of chronic abuse, however, neither time nor experience provides any corrective for this tendency toward self-blame; rather it is continually reinforced. [p. 103]

This chapter offers a different perspective from the earlier notion of the masochist seeking out a destructive partner in fantasy or reality to manage aggression toward the self, or to manage inherent incestuous strivings; this perspective replaces a focus on the patient's hostile rivalry for fear of punishment arising from an innately driven oedipal complex, with an examination of the parental environment before deciding that the self-abusive syndrome originates exclusively from the patient's drives.

The difference in theoretical perspective is exemplified behaviorally when the psychotherapist is treating a female patient who is self-abusive and seductive in her attempts to seek out and provoke abuse from others or from sadistic males in particular. If the psychotherapist's comments imply a joy in suffering, to paraphrase the title of a recent psychoanalytic text (Panken 1983), without understanding how seeking pain developed as a secondary adaptation to the primary longing for affection and love, then the clinician has repeated the interactional trauma of childhood and reinforced the patient's self-hatred and deepest conviction of her inherent badness. The therapist risks confirming the patient's dysfunctional pattern and repeating the conditions or relational trauma by focusing on the old model of innateness. This, coupled with the fact that battered women are prescribed antipsychotic drugs, pain medicine, and tranquilizers three times more often than women who are not battered, continues the emphasis on medicating symptoms rather than treating causal agents of abuse (Moss 1991).

ORIGINS OF SADISM
AND MALE DEVELOPMENT

Aggression of destructive proportions has been viewed as innate to males, just as masochism has been to females. The New York Academy of Science (Bass 1995) addressed this issue in its recent conference, "Understanding Aggressive Behavior in Children." Conference participants presented evidence that early stress alters the hormonal and neurochemical system of children permanently, and concluded that early deprivation correlated strongly with later violence. Psychologist Cathy Spatz Widom presented a 20-year study that followed 908 children who had been physically abused or neglected seriously enough for criminal charges to be filed. Those children who had been physically abused had double the rate of arrests for violent crimes than a control group, and those who had been neglected had 50 percent more arrests. Children who were not violent tended to have high IQs, high reading ability, a responsible caregiver, and had lived with both parents at some point in their lives.

Recent research indicates that children whose parents divorce, or are alcoholic, physically abusive, and have harsh rearing practices, have significantly higher rates of overt aggressive behavior than children who are not exposed to these factors (Kingston and Prior 1995, Moss and Kirisci 1995, Prino and Peyrot 1994, Vivona et al. 1995). The American Psychological Association Practice Directorate (1996) further emphasizes the role of environment in its recently released report on family violence. The report was the culmination of two years of study by a twenty-two-member multidisciplinary advisory council that substantiated the common finding that exposure to abuse, even if only as an observer, places a child at high risk of being a perpetrator or a victim of violence as an adult. Incidents of violence were more prevalent in families with four or more children. Families with incomes less than $15,000 were seven times more likely to report abuse. In families who own guns, a person is eight times as likely to kill or be killed by a family member.

Psychiatrist Jim Gilligan, in his recent book, *Violence: Our Deadly Epidemic and Its Causes* (1996), reports that after twenty-five years of interviewing convicted rapists and murderers he is convinced that violence is not caused by heredity, instinctual factors, drugs, or alcohol. He maintains that violence is more influenced by personal and social conditions, particularly poverty and the humiliations that accompany lack of financial security than by biochemical factors. The histories of excessively violent men revealed extreme childhood abuse, establishing that abuse is quite likely to breed abuse. Some individuals, however, do not follow this pattern, possibly indicating that the key difference may lie in beliefs, social interaction skills, concurrent physical vitality, and some temperamental factors.

The research cited above supports clinical data that indicate that sadism is not an expression of an innate, aggressive drive primarily, but a disintegration product of an environment that is perceived as nonresponsive. Kohut's (1977, 1984) tenet that man's destructiveness is a secondary reaction, that destructive rage is motivated by an injury to the self, is aligned with contemporary biological and societal research. In fact, recent research with positron emission tomography (PET) scans by van der Kolk and colleagues (Bass 1996b) and other neuroscientists has indicated that blood flow to the amygdala, the part of the brain that stores highly emotional memories, significantly increased during retrieval of traumatic memories, and blood flow to Broca's area, responsible for language, decreased. This finding is thought to possibly account for the difficulty traumatized individuals have putting their feelings into words, and further establishes that environmental trauma alters one's biology.

Sadism, from this perspective, can be viewed as an attempt to protect a fragile sense of self with the glue of projected aggression, rather than experience the internalized devastation of self-hatred. The individual protects himself from being hurt further by responding to perceived aggression with even greater force, thus creating false assurance that his own self-doubt will not be set in motion by external critique. Anna Ornstein (1991) recently commented on this dynamic in the psychotherapeutic interaction:

> Sadism in this context is not the product of the unmitigated aggressive drive, but the expression of chronic narcissistic rage for being repeatedly frustrated in relation to a transference need to be accepted, valued, and appreciated. The aggressive attitude has two simultaneous functions. On the one hand, it is a demand for acceptance and appreciation, not different from a child's angry demandingness when the environment is not spontaneously responsive to these developmental needs. On the other hand, anticipating the frustration of these transference needs, the aggressive attitude is also retaliatory in nature. [p. 392]

Solidification of this interpersonal method of protecting the self is fostered by cultural beliefs about masculinity. At the American Psychological Association's 1994 annual meeting, 500 researchers and clinicians attended a symposium entitled "Toward a New Psychology of Men," where a consensus was again reached that male violence cannot adequately be explained by biology, but can be explained by learned gender roles, as is clear with masochistic theories of women.

Interestingly, psychologist Vicki Helgeson (1993), who studies the relationship between gender roles and heart attacks, found that men who scored high on measures of traditional masculinity (competitiveness, hostility, achievement orientation) and women who scored high on measures of traditional femininity (self-sacrifice) had higher incidences of severe heart attacks and heart conditions, respectively. These preliminary findings may support the idea that those who have learned to adhere to the extremes of cultural stereotypes have created an imbalance that is not in their interest.

Additionally, clinical experience indicates that anger constantly thought about, repeatedly rehearsed, or felt without specific efforts to work out conflict with specific others is harmful to those with heart problems.

The benefit of outpatient group therapy modalities to address male–female cultural limitations to intimacy and self-cohesion and restriction of potential can be immeasurable.

COUNTERTRANSFERENCE GENDER DIFFERENCES

Several contemporary analytic writers have addressed countertransference difficulties. Richard Chessick (1977, 1985) and Robert Langs (1977) are representative of this group with their emphasis on the problems of seduction and chronic rage, as well as their sensitivity to the subtleties of the interpersonal field.

No author, however, has been as comprehensive in examining the psychotherapist's complex motivations as Michael Sussman in his sobering, yet critically necessary work, *A Curious Calling* (1992). Sussman cites numerous authors who have contended that "psychotherapeutic work is more congruent with the biologically and socially based roles of females than males" (p. 90). The position of the male clinician developing the feminine aspects of his personality is highlighted in his book, with emphasis on the unusual capacity of male psychotherapist for passivity and greater access to their latent femininity due to "incomplete resolution of the oedipal situation" (p. 91).

Sussman reports that much less has been written about female countertransference. However, object relations theorist Althea Horner (1979, 1990) has suggested that the role of psychotherapists allows oedipally fixated women to reconcile conflicting father–mother identifications, as this role allows women to integrate authority and empathy or, as Sussman quotes Horner, "power and femininity" (p. 94).

Other studies have indicated that the presence of strong maternal identifications drives both males and females to seek out careers in psychology and psychiatry. The characteristics cited of the father of the male psychotherapist has been less than flattering, promoting accentuation of maternal traits as defined by cultural stereotypes.

These studies represent a consensus opinion, but they use the restrictive definitions of gender roles from classical psychoanalytic and societal custom. These criteria may be insufficient for attaining optimal health.

The analytic model that links the capacity to see through the eyes of another person to gender does not hold up to contemporary clinical experiences or experimental scrutiny. One can develop the ability to empathize without any internal distortion or gender bias. It is entirely possible that empathy—defined as the ability to understand and respond to the inner world of another with the intent of fostering progressive personal development—can be experienced by men without feminine connotation, and that women can be powerful, appropriately authoritative, and empathic without being ambivalently fixated between mother–father identifications. Women and men have nonpathological desires to help and heal, based on exposure to parental figures and others. Exposure to those who possessed and exemplified the ever-important ability of interactional balance (see below), without diffusing their identities as male or female, should also be considered a crucial factor.

INTERACTIONAL BALANCE
AND THE THERAPEUTIC PROCESS

Interactional balance is defined as a manner of responding to another that exemplifies neither extreme of aggression or submission, but rather displays straightforward assertive involvement in moments of emotional intensity. This ability allows one to observe and internalize the integration of thought, emotion, and expression in a manner not biased by historic underpinnings or stereotypical gender-roles. The psychotherapist's reactive manner is balanced in terms of clarity of perception, not predicated upon prior unresolved conflict or fixed sex-role definition. Display of intensity with clarity, empathy, and firmness, is necessary in treating patients who are suffering chronically from the inability to manage their own internal tensions and impulses.

Interpretations with neutral affect are not believable to these patients as they are accustomed to words filled with emotion. Interpretations flowing with unharnessed emotion creates either false expectations or repetition of trauma through the patient's efforts to fulfill the psychotherapist's need for affirmation. Patients whose sense of self has suffered from the extremes of either parental emotional onslaught or parental cerebral detachment, or both, have little experience with a state of being at ease with themselves and, more fundamentally, they have little experience with tolerance of a mix of feelings toward self or other, without fragmentation of relationships or oneself.

Heinz Kohut (1977, 1984) has been credited with taking the word *narcissism* out of the dirty-word category, as Freud (1896) was credited with doing with the word *sex*. It is imperative that we, as psychotherapists, remove the word *ambivalence* from the dirty-word category and its association with the pejorative connotations of the word *borderline*. We must acknowledge the experience of doubt and indecision created by conflicting wishes that produce rich involvement with others when expressed and understood. *Ambivalence, sex,* and *narcissism* are not dirty words, but rather natural feelings and aspects of development that always bear the possibility of either enriching or destroying our relationships to each other and our internal dialogue.

An interchange between Barbara, a young anorexic girl in John Sours' compelling novel and text, *Starving to Death in a Sea of Objects: The Anorexia Nervosa Syndrome* (1980), and her psychiatrist shortly before Barbara dies is illustrative. Dr. Weiss asks:

"You desperately need to feel in control of all situations, don't you?"

"I sure do," Barbara said. She turned her head, then went on, raising her voice to avoid interruption. "If I'm not, then someone else will be. That's the way it's always been." She closed her eyes and gave out a tiny whimper. "I used to be a good little girl who did what my parents wanted. I always saw my mother as my best friend, my companion, even though she was usually at work. I was always well-behaved and always knew what to do. I was the nicest one in the family—certainly better than Peter [her brother]." It all came to her suddenly, with perfect clarity, as though someone next to her had whispered it into her ear. "I really wanted to impress my parents with my dieting—they never could do it as well. I could never get angry with my parents—it always made me feel so imperfect, frail. Whenever I'd get angry with them, I'd sense a voice in me telling me to behave myself, control myself before every good thing in me was lost. For me, things have to be perfect in order to be good."

"Why were you so good?"

"I was afraid . . . they wouldn't love me anymore." Her chest filled up, then her eyes.

Barbara studied the patterns in the oriental rug. She started to count its purple rings. She looked for a sign, but she knew better. But still she cried. Suddenly she straightened up like someone who had reached a decision, ready to turn on her heel and stalk out of the room. But she settled back into her chair, sobbing.

"I've always been worried my parents would die, get a divorce or stop loving me. When Peter was born, I thought I had disappointed my mother. She had exchanged me for Peter." She shuddered once, so violent she imagined her teeth rattling.

"You've worried a great deal about letting your mother down," Dr. Weiss said, her voice full of pressure.

"And I have in many ways," Barbara said, confessing. "She's fed up with me. I'm not going to complete this school year. My transcript will have withdrawals on it."

"What else has she wanted from you?" Dr. Weiss asked, as if with scorn, but only by accident.

"She always expected me to be beautiful, a Cybill Shepherd, like in *Heartbreak Kid*." Then, firmly: "But I don't want that kind of burden. And if I really start eating, I'd eat all the time. I need a voice around me telling me not to eat, warning me. The voice is always there, critical, harsh and exacting."

"You are right. You hate yourself down to your bones. You punish yourself with your worries about eating and getting fat." Dr. Weiss looked away, compressed her lips and made an entry in Barbara's chart. She looked up, wet her lips and said, "And you're paranoid."

Pure rage tore through Barbara's mind, hurling her back into her cage of doubt and misery. [pp. 177–178]

This "fictional" example highlights the repetition of trauma through the psychotherapist's description of behavior without an adequate explanation of understandable interpersonal origins. It also highlights the difficulty of experiencing this tremendous emotional torment with some semblance of balance without resorting to a position of false assuredness or to what a supervisee of mine once called "pathological certainty." Barbara gave several interpersonal cues to the origin of her thinking and to her behavior. As we follow the sequence of her communication she begins by agreeing with Dr. Weiss regarding her need for control. She explains that by being compliant, good, and "the nicest one in the family," she was able to hold onto the idea that she and her mother were best friends. She further adds, as she speaks spontaneously, that her mother was infrequently available, that she believed her dieting was impressive to her parents, and that anger was a very threatening emotion to experience. Barbara has now given critical interpersonal information in that she perceived the parental bond to be tenuous and not accepting of her as a whole person. However, she does not reveal the interpersonal origin of her fear, but rather tells the therapist how she has come to believe that love is synonymous with one's ability to perform perfectly and please others, namely her parents. Her deathly fear of separating is further emphasized as she describes how maintaining physical beauty is a burden she does not want, but, unfortunately, without her awareness she has internalized her perception of her mother's critical, harsh, and exacting voice that will not let her be free.

Barbara not only displays the interpersonal origins of self-abuse in this vignette, but also provides an opportunity to understand the interpersonal origins of rage as the psychotherapist's comments describe her self-hatred and paranoia with no plausible explanation other than that she is once again inherently bad. The interaction between patient and psychotherapist provides clear information as to how abuse to self and others originates in one's perceptual world, and how those perceptions are solidified through repetition of descriptive labeling. Instead of providing the necessary understanding of how behavioral patterns form and evolve, the psychotherapist's remarks confirm the patient's fixation of her inherent badness, which is consistent and characteristic of a child's egocentric understanding of causality. The psychiatrist, given the opportunity to enlarge and expand the patient's understanding of human relations, reinforces the developmental arrest that holds her exclusively accountable for interrelations. The psychotherapist has now repeated the failure of the parents and solidified the patient's self-hatred. This perspective does not assume that the patient's perceptions of his or her parents are accurate, but it is a perspective that begins with a concerted effort to understand the perceptions; often this process becomes the foundation from which a therapeutic alliance is formed.

Judith Herman's (1992) comments on integrity and trust aptly describes the ultimate results of the above process when it is successful:

> Integrity is the capacity to affirm the value of life in the face of death, to be reconciled with the finite limits of one's own life and the tragic limitations of the human condition, and to accept these realities without despair. Integrity is the foundation upon which trust in relationships is originally formed, and upon which shattered trust may be restored. The interlocking of integrity and trust in caretaking relationships completes the cycle of generations and regenerates the sense of human community which trauma destroys. [p. 154]

MANAGED CARE IMPLICATIONS

The advent of managed care's "medical necessity" criterion has created new pressure for psychotherapists. Communicating with the third-party insurance reviewer becomes crucial for all psychotherapists, including those treating patients with abuse histories. Any lack of clarity on the part of the psychotherapist that results in coverage being disapproved can re-create perceptions of abuse in the patient. The therapist's attitude about monetary issues becomes readily apparent, as do other countertransference issues related to rescue fantasies, authority conflicts, boundary management, and unresolved regulation of masochistic and sadistic tendencies.

The abused patient frequently longs for an idealized other who can undo the pains of the past, and create the wished-for alliance that assures the individual of being loved unconditionally. The trauma patient often feels used for some purpose, rather than loved for his or her essence. This is representative of the patient's abused childhood when parents may have used and sacrificed the child to protect their own vulnerabilities.

The sensitivities of the abused are understandably immense, which necessitates clear communication on the part of the psychotherapist, particularly regarding managed care involvement in the therapy process. Despite clarity of communication, however, patients still feel abandoned and enraged by the limitations of the insurer, and ultimately by the therapist. This emotional intensity must be dealt with directly, empathetically, and with balance so that the patient is not deprived of internalizing the psychotherapist's ability to manage intensity without

becoming overly permissive or detached. The psychotherapist is responsible not for the patient's past or for the
insurance company's provisions, but for providing an
atmosphere of empathy and dignity, and showing commitment to helping individuals understand how their past
influences current perceptions, and how they can develop
new internal sustenance to unleash potentials that have
been buried by the pains of yesterday.

∞ 2 ∞

Biopsychosocial Adjustments to the Addiction Recovery Process

The treatment of addictions has met with clinical as well as societal prejudice. Years of counterproductive debate on the role of genetic and environmental factors in the addictive cycle have cost time and money and produced only ineffective treatment. The medical community has shunned both alcoholics and illicit drug users, despite the epidemic proportions of these problems.

Today's emphasis on the biopsychosocial disease model of addiction emphasizes biological, psychological, emotional, and spiritual development with an appreciation of the complex interplay of these various factors. Despite increased acceptance of this innovative model, addicts are still difficult to treat and require much patience and understanding on their long road to recovery. They are all too frequently met with subtle or overt frustration by hospital staff when relapses occur, which are experienced by the staff as treatment failures rather than as an expected part of the recovery process.

Patients with eating disorders have met similar societal and medical prejudice. That prejudice is so strong and pervasive that many experts believe our culture's view of thinness is itself an illness. Young women face increased pressure to match *Cosmopolitan* cover models, as the ideal body shape has become thinner and thinner over the last twenty years. The risk of death from voluntary starvation has increased. The idealized quest for physical perfection continues to drive twenty million Americans onto weight loss programs. Eating disorders are extremely difficult to deal with and, like other addictions, can involve years of treatment. Their persistent symptoms remain life threatening.

The enormous complexity of these syndromes demands integrated, comprehensive, interdisciplinary approaches, while satisfying managed care criteria for brief treatment with tangible results. Overworked clinicians come to resent the additional requirements of these treatments, particularly when their understanding of the long-term recovery process may be limited. Hospital staff members frequently act out unconscious aggression toward these patients. They react to the extra needs for time, effort, and treatment coordination. Short inpatient stays, marked by intense resistance to eating normally, do not often provide personnel with a sense of efficacy, but rather represent treatment failures. Ironically, this perception is not indicative of treatment collapse, but merely marks the beginning of the complicated road to recovery.

The obese have also suffered societal and treatment bias. Programs for eating disturbances traditionally focus on anorexia and bulimia. The overweight male may escape the societal stigma obesity gives to females, but he encounters denial and prejudice from caregivers who assess and treat him; they often underestimate the severity of his symptoms. It has been relatively common in my clinical practice to receive referrals of corporate executives who are described as highly driven, anxious, and experiencing marital difficulties with no mention of their weight problems, even though they may be likely coronary and stroke victims.

Additional societal and treatment categorization promotes gender stereotypes. Clinicians need to do careful assessments to lessen the alienation of those with addictions that do not seem to fit expected gender norms. Recent research has supported linking certain variables with male alcoholism and female eating disorders. The following correlations have been found: Males—alcoholism, nicotine, and caffeine addictions; perpetration of aggression, violence, and sexual abuse. Females—eating disorders; self-abuse, perfectionistic, obsessive behavior; victims of sexual abuse—variables unique to Western women.

The prevalence of alcoholism as a male disorder is largely, but not entirely, accurate. The National Institute on Alcohol Abuse and Alcoholism (1990) estimates that there are 10.5 million Americans who are alcoholic and an additional 7.2 million are alcoholic abusers. It has been estimated that more than two-thirds of alcoholics are male, therefore 3.5 million alcoholics are female and are in need of treatment programs designed to the varying experience of their disease. The American Medical Association, in a recent media briefing on alcoholism (Foreman 1996d), announced that the long-standing gender gap in alcoholism is decreasing. Research has indicated a strong link between depression and female alcoholism. Other research indicates male problem drinkers are just 2 percent more likely to suffer from depression than nonalcoholic men. A recent study of 16,000 women at the National Institute of Environmental Health Sciences found that female social drinkers may risk increased likelihood of breast cancer. Another study demonstrated that women are particularly vulnerable to the effects of drinking because they have smaller amounts of a stomach enzyme called alcohol dehydrogenase, which helps digest alcohol (Foreman 1996b).

Caroline Knapp, in an interview regarding her recently released book, *Drinking: A Love Story* (1996), commented that it would have been very helpful if she had read something regarding a female's perspective of alcoholism:

The way women (at least women like me) use alcohol to deaden a wide range of conflicted feelings—longing for intimacy and terror of it; a wish to merge with others and a fear of being consumed; profound uncertainty about how and when to maintain boundaries and how and when to let them down. . . . Alcohol becomes infused in every aspect of your identity and your life. It's a central way of managing emotions and feelings. . . . Drinking brings out very unfemale behavior in women. It makes you more aggressive. It makes you more likely to act out sexually. You're tougher, less nurturing. It resolves conflicts for women in particular ways: how sexual to be. How assertive to be. How aggressive to be. What to act like in public. What to act like in private. It just takes all that away temporarily. . . . Sometimes women talk differently about their drinking. You'll get an emotional history from a woman—this is a generalization—and a chronological history from a man. What happened. The events of one's life, rather than this is how I felt and this is how I felt and then that's how I felt. [Sege 1996b, p. 66]

Knapp is highlighting how women tend to drink for functional, relational reasons and tend to be more representative of what has been called *milieu-limited alcoholism*. Adoption studies have established strong evidence to indicate the existence of two types of alcoholic families, one type where alcoholism is present in only male members and another type where both men and women have alcoholism. Milieu-limited alcoholism involves genetic and environmental factors whereas *male-limited alcoholism* is limited to males and has a high genetic influence and insignificant environmental influences. Milieu-limited is characterized by frequent guilt, low rates of novelty seeking, and rare violent behavior; overall, it is consistent with a passive-dependent personality structure. In contrast, the male-limited subtype is characterized by rare incidents of experienced guilt, frequent occurrences of violence and arrests, along with frequent incidents of novelty-seeking behavior; it is consistent with antisocial personality disorders. Information regarding these two subtypes of alcoholism was gleaned from Mim Landry's (1994) comprehensive and well-written text, *Understanding Drugs of Abuse.*

The remaining male-gender addiction profile is alcoholics who smoke, who have been found to drink more than alcoholics who do not smoke (York and Hirsch 1995). It was additionally discovered that smokers' intake of caffeine through coffee is higher than nonsmokers, and the correlation with heavy drinking is consistent, as opposed to those who ingest caffeine through tea, who tend to be female and lighter drinkers (Klesges et al. 1994). Overall, it is well known that heavy drinkers and alcoholics have other poor preventive health habits, such as smoking, low rates of seat belt use, and poor diet, but recovering individuals tend to reverse these trends including quitting cigarette smoking and practicing good habits associated with cardiovascular health (Silbersiepe and Hardy 1995).

It is also not surprising that males perpetrate violence and sexual abuse, and recent reports indicate that chemical dependence is present in at least half of the families who are investigated by child welfare workers for neglect and child abuse (Dore et al. 1995). In fact, heightened aggressivity has been found to be a consistent predictor of risk for an alcohol disorder in adulthood, particularly as pertains to adolescent aggression and alcoholism (Moss and Kirisci 1995). Alcoholic men with the personality trait of hypermasculinity judge violent pornography to be more positive, further substantiating the obvious relationship among aggressivity, alcohol abuse, and violent behavior (Norris and Kerr 1993). This collection of behaviors has been found to be primarily male based, although not exclusively. Nevertheless, societal and clinical expectations, particularly the perceptions of family members of alcoholics and those of behavioral medicine practitioners, are based on the validity of the above-cited data.

The societal stigma may be greater for female alcoholics, but both sexes face perceptions that can be particularly difficult to overcome, making support of peers a critical aspect in long-term recovery. Male recovering alcoholics and substance abusers have much to overcome in order to change expectations so that current behavior can eventually override past addiction-associated behaviors.

The obvious societal and medical alcohol characteriza-
tion applies most often to male-limited alcoholism, leaving male and female alcoholics who do not fit this subtype in a less understood position. A recent addictions
conference at Harvard Medical School featured several
specialists who have come to believe that significant reliance on the biomedical model may account for the high
rates of failure in most treatment programs, including
Alcoholics Anonymous (AA), where some studies claim
a 50 percent dropout rate (Bass 1996a). The biomedical
model, consistent with male-limited alcoholism, has
greatly aided in dispelling biases regarding previous myths
that described the addict as amoralistic and lacking willpower. In addition, the disease model has allowed for
better access to medical and psychological care, but our
advancing knowledge indicates that this care is not appropriate for all who suffer from alcohol-related disturbances.

Patients with eating disorders have been characterized
as females who are perfectionistic, self-abusive (masochistic), obsessive, sexually abused, and a product of Western culture. Although these characterizations are often
accurate, we must carefully examine clinical and research
data to find treatment plans that facilitate recovery without unnecessary complications. In addition, it is imperative to remember that descriptive diagnosis addresses
general symptom groups, not the internal, unique experience of the individual. Nevertheless, it is necessary to
clarify and differentiate statistical and research data to aid

the recovering person in understanding both the clinical and research information that influences treatment program design and societal impression. For instance, anorexia has been estimated to develop in one of every 200 adolescents between the ages of 12 and 18, with 90 percent being females, while the incidence of males being affected has increased from 5 percent in 1985 to 10 percent in 1987 (Romeo 1994). It is also estimated that bulimia affects 10 to 15 percent of the male population, and it is likely that the prevailing view of eating disorders as being female disorders has prevented males from acknowledging this problem. It has also been speculated that males with eating disorders struggle with an assortment of sexual difficulties that may further inhibit disclosing their overall suffering to a professional (Aronson 1993).

Underlying personality disorders have been consistent with poor prognosis for eating disorders, with obsessive-compulsive personality being common to those suffering from bulimia and anorexia (Rastman et al. 1995). There is a higher incidence of borderline personality and alcohol and substance abuse in bulimics than in anorexics, who in turn have a high incidence of anxiety disorder, avoidant personality, and perfectionism (Bastiani et al. 1995, Holderness et al. 1994, Skodol et al. 1993). Incidents of sexual abuse are significant among eating disorders, with some studies indicating the highest statistical rates among bulimics and the obese (deGroot et al. 1992, Waller 1993). Lauren Slater, a psychologist, whose recent book, *Welcome to My Country* (1996), details her own account of developing and recovering from bulimia, renders this individualized view in an interview regarding her experience of abuse:

> Abuse is too facile an explanation for emotional trauma, so when she [Slater] talks about her childhood she talks about the constant, constant fear of abuse that was akin to living in a state of terror, and about her family's dynamic of humiliation before she mentions getting socked, getting punched, dragged by your hair and all that stuff. People focus nowadays on the abuse. "What happened?" "What did this person actually do to you?" "What really stands out in my mind is the quality of being humiliated, verbally, over and over and over again." . . . One morning after her fifth hospitalization, Slater awoke with a 'vision of myself as I truly was, and I suddenly knew this was not who I was supposed to be, that I have taken a wrong turn somewhere and this woman I had become was an aberration." [Sege 1996a, p. 90]

Caroline Knapp, cited earlier, also poignantly describes her individualized reaction to the interplay between food and alcohol addictions in a recent interview with the same journalist. At heart, she says,

> "All addictions are driven by the same impulses and most accomplish the same goals; you just use a different substance, or take a slightly different path to get there. For

women, that path often winds around alcohol and heads straight through food. You hear about women who became bulimic or anorexic in high school or college, then established some kind of equilibrium around food when or after they started drinking. . . . It's more tempting to relapse into anorexia," Knapp says. "It's more subtle. You pick up a drink and you've had a relapse. You eat weirdly one day, and is that a relapse? It's much murkier. I'm scared enough about a relapse with drinking that I'll go to great lengths to avoid it, but food is something you have to make decisions about many times each day." [Sege 1996b, p. 66]

The tenuous aspects of recovery from addictions, as cited above, are further aggravated by the physical complications of alcoholism, substance abuse, and eating difficulties. It has been long documented that alcoholism leaves the body and mind stressed to levels that cannot easily be revived. Malnutrition, organ damage, neurochemical imbalances, immunological disorders, and neurological and endocrine abnormalities are profound as alcoholism progresses, and their effects are often underestimated in terms of complications of treatment (Beasley 1989). The reader is referred to the comprehensive texts of Jerome Levin (1987, 1995) for detailed accounts of the somatic illnesses associated with alcohol abuse, as well as for detailed accounts of the recovery process through AA involvement and intensive psychotherapy. Levin, an expert in the addiction field, demonstrates the wisdom of a seasoned clinician in terms of treating the various personas of alcoholism and substance abuse. His understanding of the biopsychosocial model of addiction is comprehensive and highly informative. The following excerpt from his recent book (1995) briefly summarizes the potential physiological effects of alcoholism:

> Alcohol abuse can damage any part of the body. The damage may be direct, the consequence of alcohol's effect on a particular cell, tissue, organ, or system, or it may be indirect, the consequence of alcohol's profound alteration of the body's internal chemical environment. The most common sites of damage are the nervous system, liver, and blood. The gastrointestinal system, heart, muscles, and reproductive organs also may be damaged.
>
> Although the mechanisms by which alcohol destroys cells and damages organs are multiple, complex, and only partly understood, it is believed that alcohol's ability to penetrate membranes and disrupt membrane phenomena leads to cell death and is one of the most important pathways to somatic damage secondary to alcohol abuse. [p. 37]

Additionally, researchers have recently found that alcoholic women have a shorter life span (Hill 1995), while their children are of significantly lower birth weights (Dobkin et al. 1994), as well as being of shorter stature. Nevertheless, alcoholics in recovery do tend to use preventive health practices, including quitting smoking and maintaining overall good cardiovascular health (Silber-siepe and Hardy 1995). The process by which alcoholics become invested in overall health is quite gradual, however, and is consistently correlated with an evolving sense of a self that possesses worth and life purpose. This gradual evolution is fostered initially through psycho-educational methods of treatment that provide concrete guidance and necessary information, while later stages of recovery are more adaptable to psychodynamic work, as increasing sobriety allows for greater tolerance of affect without as great a threat of "picking up."

The medical complications of anorexia and bulimia affect the metabolic, gastrointestinal, cardiovascular, renal, fluid, electrolyte, hemamatological, and endocrine systems and can also involve dental problems. Bulimics additionally suffer from complications of laxative abuse, which causes changes in skin pigmentation, fluid retention, malabsorption syndromes, and protein loss, as well as other complications. The obese also suffer increased likelihood of several diseases, such as coronary heart disease, diabetes mellitus, digestive diseases, gallbladder disease, arthritis, and gout (Browell and Foreyt 1986).

In my experience, it is the anorexic who displays the greatest change in terms of cognitive clarity and availability for psychotherapy when nutritional stability is resumed. Talking to a nutritionally deprived anorectic is akin to talking to an alcoholic at a bar—distortions abound. It has been proven through experimental starvation that individuals without disorders will develop the common symptoms of anorexia such as irritability, depression, concentration difficulties, and obsessive thinking, but do not develop the anorexic's fear of food and body image distortions. The reader is referred to Browell and Foreyt's text *Handbook of Eating Disorders* (1986) for a comprehensive discussion of the physiological aspects of obesity, anorexia, and bulimia. Of note are several recent studies that have focused on the anorexic's propensity for osteoporosis with accompanying stress fractures (LaBan et al. 1995), bone loss (Maugars and Prost 1994), and thyroid disease (Tiller et al. 1994).

The origins of eating disorders, alcoholism, and substance abuse may differ in gender and genetics, but the addictive life-style eventually makes its victims unable to manage internal thoughts and feelings, and disrupts their interpersonal relationships. Conflict due to perceptions of difference or disapproval frequently precipitates internal states that immediately reinforce and re-stimulate desires to return to the addictive cycle. This dynamic, no doubt, is what leads many addiction specialists to use psycho-educational modalities exclusively so as not to threaten the fragile state of early recovery. This stance is certainly understandable in initial treatment, but it is my contention that the addict's overall inability to maintain closeness and connection with others is the driving force to maintaining addictive behavior, and unless altered, will determine whether or not the individual will remain vulnerable to relapse.

The ability to maintain closeness with others is both self-sustaining and life giving, and, in many ways, is in harmony with the twelve steps of Alcoholics Anonymous. The skill, however, of being able to be close in a reciprocal relationship demands a solid sense of self that is developed through many interactions involving fairness, love, and consistency with individuals who relate with the interactional balance detailed in the previous chapter. Washton and Boundy (1989) aptly describe intimacy problems of those with addictions in their text *Willpower Is Not Enough: Recovery from Addictions of Every Kind.*

> The person at high risk for addiction suffers from a gnawing sense of loneliness deep within. Out of touch with herself, unable to set boundaries, needing to control, she cannot be authentic with others and cannot form lasting, gratifying bonds. This trait is not always apparent, however, because the addictive person may appear outgoing, have a lot of friends, and even be married. Generally, though, the level of intimacy in his relationships is limited—based on superficials or on mutual dependency rather than mutual sharing. So while addicts may have the outer appearance of connectedness, most describe having profound feelings of isolation deep within. The addictive involvement, then, comes to substitute for intimacy—because in

many ways addiction is a . . . relationship. The addict is often as preoccupied with his drug as a lover is with the object of his dreams; he may seem to love, honor, and protect the supply of his drug more than he does the people in his household. That's because the drug provides feelings of connectedness with others—without the demands of real intimacy. Or, in the case of a downer drug like food, heroin, and sometimes alcohol, it can numb a person from his isolation. [pp. 83–84]

The authors emphasize the lack of a sense of belonging as a prime aspect of the addict's isolation as his relationships to family and community are generally quite compromised. They see this as consistent with our self-centered culture in which relational integrity is viewed as secondary to obtaining power and maintaining image. This is thought to promote attraction to pseudocommunities based on addictive similarities such as the barroom, the racetrack, and the crack house.

Interactional group psychotherapy of patients with mixed or like addictions can successfully address the addicted person's fragile sense of self and provide a means by which the individual can begin developing an internal structure that will allow for difference, conflict tolerance, and resolution when possible. Most important, this group approach develops the capacity to remain stable when desired resolution is not possible. The desire to change one's mood through a substance or behavior gradually decreases as the psychotherapist provides the five necessary ingredients for change: empathy, interactional balance, tension management, the opportunity for internalization of the therapist's reactive style, and interpretation of behavior that brings previously hidden determinants of behavior into conscious awareness. These concepts will be elaborated in detail in Chapter 3.

The one glaring similarity of people prone to addictive lifestyles is their inordinate sensitivity to conflict. Many years of leading group therapy sessions have provided me with an opportunity to observe and participate in what are now viewed as classic examples of adaptations to conflict sensitivity. The now common occurrence of the eating-disordered female patient trying valiantly to calm and appease the male alcoholic as he displays aggression is both representative and healing when the precipitants are understood through the foundation of therapeutic empathy. It is most often the timid anorexic patient striving for perfection in an effort to appease her self-hatred who cannot tolerate the aggressive impulsivity displayed. She must be helped both to understand her fears and their historical basis, which the group interaction uncovers, and to assert herself, while running the risk of not being able to control the reaction of the demanding parent symbol. The bulimic patient is generally not as concerned as the anorexic with diluting the aggression in the room and, in fact, may join the aggressor, depending on her level of personality disturbance. As indicated earlier, these are generalizations that do not cover the range of diagnostic possibilities; nevertheless, the bulimic tends to have more in common with the alcoholic and substance abuser, such as impulsivity, abuse histories, substance abuse, and a propensity for projected aggression. The anorexic initially internalizes and ultimately acts out conflict through the private avenue of food restriction, and seldom realizes that her obsession with food is relationally based in that it is initially a nondetectable means of expression of anger, disagreement, and any other affect that is not felt to be safe to express to another. On the other hand, the male-limited alcoholic projects aggression and denies that his internal state has been threatened. The recovery work for this individual entails experiencing vulnerability as a natural state appropriate to certain situations, rather than as a flaw that will inevitably be used to humiliate. In essence, past conflict and consequent character structure are challenged in the therapeutic present as an inaccurate foundation for present perceptions.

The origin of addictions differs, as stated previously, but the ultimate therapeutic work centers on the deep pessimism that is experienced when the individual is in conflict with another. All individuals need the emotional resonance of others, but the addicted individual has lost faith in this possibility. This pessimism is based on many failed early interactions where developmental needs went unsatisfied and misunderstood. As a result, a fragile sense of self developed, rather than a secure internal structure that can tolerate difference and work through interpersonal conflict without feeling unduly threatened and ultimately without falling apart inside. Recovery from all addictions then becomes an opportunity to grow from the point where development was arrested and addictive behavior became the temporary soothing agent to lessen anxieties associated with the past. The addictive cycle then breeds impatience, with the typical steps of learning discarded as they are viewed as symbols of displayed inadequacy, rather than perceived as a normative process that takes time and the willingness to be vulnerable.

The recovery process offers, for the first time for many, the possibility of abandoning the addictive substance or behavior that initially was used for soothing anxiety and insecurity, and ultimately became the means by which negative self-perceptions were solidified and hope for one's future was destroyed. The recovery process, however, is more complicated than the self-help books and tapes describe. Addictions and addictive behavior can make individuals act similarly when in fact, from a broader understanding of personality, no two anorexic or alcoholic individuals are the same. The biopsychosocial origins of each individual's addiction must be assessed.

We have briefly examined the possible variations of alcoholic and eating disorder disturbances as the general models most often used do not always apply; in fact, they help create a rationale for returning to addictive behaviors when applied erroneously. Assuming that a bulimic

individual can be helped by following protocols established from descriptive diagnosis that is symptom based
is akin to treating depression from a biochemical frame-
work without addressing the varied origins of depression,
such as familial and socially learned behavior.

The biopsychosocial model is akin to holism in that
both conceptualizations represent an attempt to view individuals in their entirety rather than through a narrow
lens. Mim Landry (1994), in his recent text on drug abuse,
indicates that one of the most important breakthroughs
in the field of addiction treatment may be the awareness
that addiction is a multivaried disease. This emphasis on
holism and the treatment of the emotional, biological,
spiritual, and interactional elements of disturbances helps
the patient achieve better health and a renewed sense of
self by moving between narrow self perspectives.

Emphasis on the whole of a person's experience decreases guilt in that a deeper understanding of one's behavior is rendered, often resulting in a more understanding view of oneself rather than the typical vacillation from
self-flagellation to self-aggrandizement that is characteristic of the addicted person. The medium of group psychotherapy is ideal for developing wholeness because one's
fixed views of oneself and others are examined in a manner that leads to a wider perspective. The individual experiences more than recovery from particular addictions; he
experiences the recovery of lost or underdeveloped aspects
of himself.

❧ 3 ❧

Group Psychotherapy:
Outcome Studies,
Group Composition,
Therapeutic Perspectives—
A Literature Review

We have psychologically evolved as a society. We have shifted from preoccupation with inhibition and restricted expression to a culture that lacks interpersonal resonance and ultimately the sustained love of others. We have moved from a preoccupation with forbidden wishes and impulses to a growing desire for interpersonal warmth and relatedness. This shift is reflected in the emergence of group psychotherapy. The emphasis has changed from learning about oneself through individual exploration and telling of one's story to learning about oneself from intense, personal interactions. The emphasis has changed from historical searching to experience in the present that spontaneously reveals the aspects of an individual's relatedness and its qualities of joy, anxiety, peace, frustration, anger, and ultimately self-cohesion or self-fragmentation. We have moved, in essence, from Freud's world of sexual and aggressive inhibition to our current world of unbridled expression mixed with relational alienation and deadness. The late psychoanalyst Heinz Kohut (1977, 1984) insightfully described our society as experiencing a transition from an overly close nuclear family that could, when boundaries were unprotected, produce "Guilty Man," to our estranged society with lack of relational connection that results in the experience of "Tragic Man." The sustaining influence of family, religion, and state has been remarkably diminished and consequently has created an even greater desire for interpersonal meaning and sustenance (Klein et al. 1992).

Freud's initial formulations on groups and group psychotherapy focused on how individuals merge with group norms and take on a group identity, with loss of their own identity in the process. He associated a lack of autonomy with group formation, and was convinced that ingenuity is reserved for those working in solitude rather than in conjunction with others (Freud 1921). Freud's convictions applied to an early developmental stage when psychological differentiation from another has not been established, whether because of age or because of a trauma that arrested development and prevented movement from a state of psychological merger.

Contemporary group psychotherapy does not differ with these conceptualizations in early stage group treatment. The difference in perspective is more apparent in the expected developmental progression from an undifferentiated sense of self that is threatened, if not fragmented, by separating, to a differentiated sense of self that can maintain individuality and significant connection to others without fragmentation.

This chapter reviews the group therapy outcome literature and, most important, details the therapeutic process by which the above developmental progression is facilitated. The chapter describes the facilitation of the journey from a fragile, undifferentiated self prone to addictive and abusive lifestyles to an internal sense of self that is differentiated and psychologically separate from others, yet is capable of maintaining intimacy, health, and closeness without a loss of identity.

Individuality, from this perspective, can be maintained as a result of the development of a solid sense of self through interactions of appropriate assertion, affection, and validation, with a foundation of safety through reasonable adult-to-child boundaries. Ideally, this development takes place in childhood. In our culture, however, the psychotherapist often provides the interactive element that was never successfully provided by the parents, or was given in a psychologically unhealthy manner.

In recent years several theorists have attempted to discover and describe the most effective means of conducting inpatient and outpatient group psychotherapy. Although this body of outcome literature is still evolving

(Allen and Bloom 1994, Erickson 1981, Getter et al. 1992, Greene and Cole 1991, Hamilton et al. 1993, Kibel 1981, Leszcz et al. 1985b, Marcovitz and Smith 1983, Mitchell et al. 1993, Scheidlinger 1994, Tschuschke and Dies 1994), there have been several recommendations made regarding the makeup of such groups and the therapeutic stance to take.

This review of the group psychotherapy literature discusses three areas of disagreement among group researchers: (1) results of outcome studies, (2) homogeneous versus heterogeneous groups, (3) insight (psychodynamic) versus supportive (educative) psychotherapy. This discussion is integrated with a group model developed at MetroWest Medical Center in Natick, Massachusetts that is designed to increase understanding of the interactional origins of abuse, addiction, and a fragile sense of self. This model also highlights the interactional elements necessary for recovery through the development of an internal sense of cohesion that will not fragment easily and thus not result in aggressive or addictive behavior.

OUTCOME STUDIES

Several authors have examined outcome studies attempting to determine the efficacy of inpatient and outpatient psychotherapy groups. Kanas (1985) states, "In a review of 40 controlled studies, group therapy was judged to be superior to a no group therapy condition in 70 percent of the inpatient studies and 80 percent of the outpatient studies. Long-term inpatient groups were more effective than intermediate and short-term inpatient groups. Interactional-oriented approaches were more effective than insight-oriented approaches, which proved harmful for some schizophrenics in two studies" (p. 431).

Maxmen (1984), on the other hand, reports, "The evidence supporting the efficacy of group therapy for psychiatric inpatients [is] disappointing. . . . Collectively these results suggest that for treating hospitalized patients, either the methods for evaluating inpatient groups are inadequate; no type of group works; or more loosely structured, psychoanalytically oriented groups are ineffective, but other models might be worthwhile" (p. 355).

The reviews cited in the group literature of Stotsky and Zolik (1965) and Parloff and Dies (1977) covered a 52-year period collectively, with the authors concluding that group therapy is not particularly effective with significantly disturbed people. More recently, Scheidlinger (1994), in his review of nine decades of group psychotherapy, concluded that group therapy research lagged far behind the growing popularity of the practice, but he expected that managed care will provide the needed motivation to integrate research and practice. Dies and Teleska (1993) surveyed 156 group psychotherapy investigators in 29 countries, reaching the conclusion that group research has been impeded by global assessment tools and exclusive reliance on self-report. Several theorists had reached this general conclusion in the 1970s and 1980s, but believed that questioning group participants to ascertain key factors regarding their experience would produce empirical data (Leszcz et al. 1985b, Marcovitz and Smith 1983, Maxmen 1973).

Regarding the key factors ascertained, Maxmen (1984) reports that "one hundred inpatients on a short-term unit found the most helpful factors were (in order) installation of hope, group cohesiveness, altruism, and universality" (p. 360). He further reports that his findings were replicated twice (Becker and Kolit 1980, Emrick and Silver 1974) as an attestation of their reliability. Maxmen (1984) then designed an educative model to accentuate the factors mentioned above. This design will be highlighted later in this chapter.

Marcovitz and Smith (1983) conducted a study of thirty inpatients judged to be high functioning with diagnoses of primary affective disorder (sixteen), borderline or other character disorder (ten), neurosis (one), and schizophrenia (three). The relevance of this study, for our purposes, is that the instrument that was utilized was Yalom's (1975) Curative Factor Q Sort, which Yalom initially implemented with twenty neurotic or character disordered patients who had completed an average of sixteen months of outpatient group psychotherapy. Maxmen (1973) utilized a short form of this device in his inpatient study, which allowed Marcovitz and Smith (1983) to compare their effort with the Maxmen and Yalom studies. The Q Sort is described by Marcovitz and Smtih as, "a forced choice ranking of items into various normally distributed categories" (p. 23). The results indicate that 86 percent of the participants found the group helpful. In terms of the twelve curative factors ranked, "the one factor that consistently ranks in the top four is cohesiveness. . . . Catharsis and self-understanding rank high in both our study and Yalom's study. . . . Altruism is ranked in the top four in our study and Maxmen's study. . . . Factors that rank high in only one out of the three studies are inter-personal learning output (ours), installation of hope (Maxmen's), and universality (Maxmen's)" (p. 27). The authors conclude that the divergence of results regarding the two inpatient studies and the similarity of their results to Yalom's outpatient group are due to differences in theoretical orientation. They characterize their approach and Yalom's as psychodynamic, and Maxmen's as behavioral and less anxiety producing.

Interestingly, group outcome results utilizing the Q Sort (curative factors) and more contemporary measures render similar results prior to the advent of managed care and thereafter. Leszcz and colleagues (1985b) studied fifty-one inpatients hospitalized for an average of twenty-one days. Every patient in this study was required to attend an unstructured heterogeneous group that met for 75 minutes, five times weekly, and was called Team Group. A second voluntary group, the Level Group, was voluntary and attended by high-functioning patients. This group met for 75 minutes, four times weekly, and "focused primarily on a here-and-now interactional model of group therapy" (p. 413). Each patient was asked to rank order modalities of treatment and to rank order ten curative factors.

Both psychotherapy groups were ranked high and 25 percent of participants ranked group therapy first. Interestingly, patients diagnosed as borderline rated the Level Group first, major affective disorders rated individual therapy first, and patients with depressive reactions rated the homogeneous groups quite high. Schizophrenics much preferred the "less intensely interactive Team Group to the Level Group" (p. 426).

It was further reported that the heterogeneous Team Group rankings were most unlike outpatient groups with a "high valuation of hope, advice, and altruism and low valuation of interpersonal learning, vicarious learning, and self-understanding" (p. 428). The authors concluded that "hope is a developmentally early group therapeutic factor [that] resonate[s] with a need to be encouraged at a time of crisis and desperation" while "self-understanding is a mature therapeutic factor requiring more time in treatment for patient exploration and working through than is available on the acute unit" (p. 428).

Greene and Cole (1991) in their study of fifty-one inpatients, reaffirmed earlier findings that borderline patients prefer unstructured interpersonal group therapy, as opposed to psychotic patients who prefer psychoeducational structured situations, as ambiguity is experienced as emotional disaster. Utilizing a semantic differential form, the authors concluded:

> The nonpsychotic patient whose reality testing is relatively intact is thought to be well suited for a comparatively unstructured psychotherapy group, where the work is precisely the experiencing and learning about the primitive material that inevitably emerges within the group from the externalizing process of its members. But for the psychotic patient, for whom the primary aim is to facilitate the development of fundamental self–other boundaries, an ambiguous clinical situation is considered countertherapeutic. [p. 501]

Getter and colleagues (1992) employed the Group Sessions Rating Scale (GSRS) to assess ninety-six outpatients who joined an interactional therapy group or a coping skills group based on cognitive-behavioral principles. Participants had recently been discharged from a twenty-one-day inpatient alcohol and drug abuse facility. Results were parallel to those of psychotic patients in the previous study:

> Only education and skill training correlated with fewer group members reporting drinking-related problems. Moreover, contrary to our expectations, two activities considered to be essential to interactional therapy were associ-

ated with a greater percentage of group members reporting drinking-related problems. This suggests that newly ab-
stinent alcoholics in our study were not ready to manage
effectively the consequences of intensive here-and-now interaction and heightened emotional expression. [p. 428]

Allen and Bloom (1994) report on the limited research
assessing outcome of group psychotherapy with patients
suffering from posttraumatic stress disorder (PTSD) and
caution, as with the psychotic and alcoholic, that

> group and family work must be carefully considered and
> sensitively timed to avoid possible reinforcement of mal-
> adaptive patterns. . . . Depending on the integrity of
> the traumatized individual's psychological resources, the
> issues of safety and trust may best be met initially in indi-
> vidual psychotherapy. A gradual exposure to group psy-
> chotherapy should be considered. Too rapid movement
> into group psychotherapy may overwhelm impaired re-
> sources, producing secondary traumatization. [p. 427]

The authors do not rule out psychodynamic group
therapy, but encourage careful assessment of personality structure, with exposure techniques being "contraindicated by marked psychological dysfunction, personality disorder, suicidality, impulsiveness, substance abuse,
or treatment resistance" (p. 428).

Tschuschke and Dies (1994) conducted an exhaustive
study of inpatient group psychotherapy utilizing curative

factor rankings as well as several other measurements (Symptom Checklist, Global Assessment Scale, Kelly Repertory Grid, etc.). Their findings confirmed earlier outcome reports in that perceived group cohesiveness differentiated successful from unsuccessful patients in both groups studied. Self-disclosure was significantly correlated with patient report cohesiveness, while the group leader's activity level in terms of facilitating a supporting learning environment where problematic interpersonal styles are confronted and interpreted was seen as a key factor in increasing quality and depth of feedback among group members. Hamilton and his colleagues (1993) at the Houston VA Medical Center developed the Group Psychotherapy Rating Scale to build on previous work of Dies and Teleska (1985) that discussed the detrimental effects of group leaders' actions on curative factors. Their work is based on the premise that "ensuring high quality in the process of conducting group therapy and integrating the group work into the total treatment plan would tend to produce a good outcome. Research in group therapy supports the relation of process measures to outcome" (p. 319). The authors found that there are no accounts of monitoring ongoing psychotherapy as a means of quality assessment and thus their rating scale provides the opportunity to distinguish professional staff from trainees. Immediately following group sessions, therapists are given results of the rating scale, observer suggestions are made, and group therapists failing to meet established criteria are offered in-service training.

One additional finding is that outcome measures, such as curative factor rankings, are indicative of the patient population served, and those suffering from character disorders tend to respond with characteristic disappointment. Hays (1995) administered a battery of psychological tests to psychiatric inpatients within 24 hours after admission, prior to discharge, and patients were contacted at one, three, and twelve months postdischarge.

> Personality style influences responses to treatment modalities during a course of short-term hospitalization, contributes to perceptions of the general treatment environment, and impacts on patients' perceived functional and clinical status at discharge. More characerologically impaired patients, as assessed by a pattern of clinical elevations on the antisocial, avoidant, borderline, self-defeating, drug abuse, passive-aggressive and schizotypal scales on the Millon Clinical Multiaxial Inventory-11, were at high risk to report that they did not receive the help they needed during the short-term hospitalization. These non-responders to treatment were a younger group than patients who reported that they received the help they needed. They remained in the hospital two days longer than the Helped group. As might be expected, they had higher recidivism rates. This Not Helped group utilized more resources with minimal benefits when compared to the Help group. Treatment of the non-responder in a short-term hospital stay is not cost-effective. [p. 24]

Hays goes on to say that although clinician competence is an important variable in the outcome success equation, underlying personality features of the patient population are critical to interpreting outcome measures accurately.

It is evident, nevertheless, that researchers who utilized Yalom's (1975) curative factor rank technique, and other various measures, do conclude that group therapy is viewed positively by most patients. The research collectively indicates that what is considered helpful depends on the level of disturbance of individual patients, as well as the therapeutic stance emphasized by group leaders. There is a divergence of opinion regarding group composition (heterogeneous versus homogeneous) and choice of modality (insight/psychodynamic versus supportive/ educative), as discussed in the following section.

HOMOGENEOUS VERSUS HETEROGENEOUS GROUPS

Several theorists have recommended homogeneous group therapy for selected diagnostic categories as well as age-specific groupings (e.g., adolescent, elderly). Group therapy for schizophrenics has been advocated most often (Betcher et al. 1982, Drake et al. 1993, Kahn 1984, Kahn and Kahn 1992, Kanas 1985, Leszcz et al. 1985b, Serok et al. 1984, Wexler et al. 1984), and, to a lesser degree, there has been a call for clinicians to utilize homogenous group modalities for individuals with borderline and narcissistic personality disorders (Buchele 1994, Kibel 1978, Klein et al. 1991, Slavinsky-Holly 1980, 1983, 1988, Spotnitz 1957, Wong 1980), eating disorders (Aronson 1993, Goodsitt 1985, Hall 1985, Mitchell et al. 1993), posttraumatic stress disorder (Buchele 1994, Zaidi 1994), manic-depression (Kanas 1993, Volmar et al. 1981), alcoholics (Blume 1978, Flores and Mahon 1993, Landry 1994, Levin 1995, Vannicelli 1982, Vannicelli et al. 1984, Yalom 1974), postpartum depression (Gruen 1993), adolescent disturbances (Beeferman and Orvaschel 1994, Bernfield et al. 1984, Brandes and Moosbruger 1984, Hurst and Gladieux 1980, Rachan and Raubolt 1984), and the depressed elderly (Berger et al. 1972, Clark and Vorst 1994, Cooper 1981, Johnson et al. 1985, Leszcz et al. 1985a, Liberman and Bliwise 1985, Zerhusen et al. 1991).

The benefit derived from homogeneous groupings for the above disturbances is that commonality of suffering can foster group cohesion and elicit hope, as AA has shown. However, I believe that heterogeneous groups can complement diagnosis-oriented groups in an inpatient setting, and offer an opportunity for enhanced interpersonal interactions, not just stabilization of the initial presenting disturbance. In certain instances heterogeneous groups may be the treatment of choice, for example for relational difficulties that result in pronounced interpersonal distress.

The mixed-diagnoses group provides a "real life" environment with its diverse transferences and their resultant complexities. Heterogeneous outpatient groups can be quite effective when participants are selected for having similar internal structure while manifesting diverse symptom representation. Counseling centers with comprehensive group programs ideally facilitate movement from diagnosis-oriented psychoeducational groups to intensive interactional groups as patients stabilize and can tolerate and benefit from more in-depth exploration of chronic self-defeating behavioral patterns. Inpatient mixed groups, when managed effectively, can significantly contribute to cohesion within the milieu, and to the idea that it is possible to relate to varied groups of people outside the hospital (internalization of hope). The ability to relate to and understand others is important for all people, but it is especially consequential for those with preoedipal disturbances who experience intense anxiety with interpersonal closeness.

Schizophrenics

This line of thinking is used to support the opposite conclusion by some therapists to exclude schizophrenics from mixed groups. Kanas (1985) aptly represents this posture by making the following points regarding schizophrenics in mixed inpatient or outpatient groups: (1) healthier patients scapegoat sicker patients in group, (2) cohesion is difficult to develop when ego functioning varies, (3) needs of patients are difficult to meet if symptoms and interpersonal ability differ, (4) problems of technique are likely as techniques helpful for one patient may be counterproductive for another, (5) schizophrenics regress when uncovering and self-disclosure are group norms.

While these concerns are legitimate, whether or not these problems occur depends on the group leader's experience and therapeutic perspective (to be discussed in the next section), the patient's medications, and specific treatment plans and their implementation. If a good treatment plan is in effect, the patient may do better in a mixed group. For example, a schizophrenic patient stabilized on medication can usually participate well in mixed groups. Instead of decreasing group cohesiveness, the schizophrenic's participation can lift group spirit, since most fellow patients sense the level of anxiety such patients live with, and consequently view appropriate contributions from the more disturbed as hopeful. Arieti (1974) comments on hospitalization after the schizophrenic has established relatedness with a staff therapist: "After accepting the therapist the patient generally accepts the therapeutic assistant, a nurse, or some other person. His milieu and realm of action become more diversified; the interchange less stereotyped. There is less rigidity in the psychological structure and the patterns of behavior are less repetitive" (p. 556).

Schizophrenics who have ongoing relationships, particularly with individual or group therapists, are more likely to take medication and remain in contact with others. Kahn (1984), in a succinct review, cited nonpharmacologic therapies for schizophrenics from a number of studies that demonstrate the value of socially oriented interventions that improve quality and satisfaction of life for these patients. He cites the shift from the interpersonal to somatic therapies that occurred in the mid-1950s and the recent recognition that medication alone is not comprehensive treatment for the schizophrenic. Frank (1975) states, "Schizophrenics, like diabetics, require drugs, but they also need long-term psychotherapeutic support to enable them to function to the limit of their capacities" (p. 149). Kahn (1984) further comments that outpatient group therapy for schizophrenia has been supported in the literature as a treatment that improves medication compliance, reduces hospitalization, and ultimately improves social and occupational abilities. Others have concurred with this optimism: "For many patients, group therapy is their primary socializing experience, and it is amazing how high attendance can be. Some studies have found attendance rates to reach 95% or higher. In our previously cited study, the attendance rate was 88%" (Kanas 1985, p. 437). "Clinic attendance in general for schizophrenia has been found to be from 71 to 86%, especially when phone prompts are utilized" (Carrion et al. 1993).

Some are concerned about mixed grouping because schizophrenics have at times, especially upon admission, fostered regression in similarly disturbed individuals in the inpatient milieu. As Mosher and Gunderson (1979) have pointed out regarding group composition: "There should be some range of over disturbance; that is, a group composed exclusively of very disturbed individuals will make it more difficult for any of them to learn from another member how to cope more effectively" (p. 413). It has also been observed that schizophrenics' initial expressions of affect, especially anxiety, are quite threatening to other group members. Nonpsychotic patients talk of their inability to understand and consequently empathize with such unfamiliar experiences. They are in essence experiencing the parallel difficulty that psychotherapists have in making sense of primitive verbalizations. It is at these moments that the group as a whole turns subtly to the group leader, and the leader's empathic range is tested. Group anxiety will be lessened or heightened depending on the nature of the intervention. If managed successfully, healthier patients will often acknowledge their resistance to understanding (i.e., "I'm afraid I'll go crazy") and the schizophrenic patient is calmed momentarily through the leader's ability to communicate understanding while decreasing the patient's perception of fear. Some group members will inevitably follow the leader's approach to the schizophrenic, his example being perceived as encouraging others to risk closeness with the more disturbed members. Identification with being the "sick person" and the scapegoated person in one's family is also a characteristic comment of nonpsychotic patients at these times.

In summary, the schizophrenic patient can benefit from the mixed inpatient group when he or she is stabilized on medication, and the precipitants of the patient's condition are addressed, because relational opportunities are available and milieu estrangement is avoided. The outpatient group demands adherence to similar selection criteria.

Borderlines and Narcissists

Group therapy has also been recommended for those patients diagnosed with borderline and narcissistic disturbances. Divergent views have been expressed regarding the inclusion or exclusion of these patients (Buchele 1994, Elbirik et al. 1994, Greene and Cole 1991, Klein et al. 1991, Slavinsky-Holly 1980, 1983, 1988, Wong 1980) in group composition. Wong (1980) cautioned that groups exclusive to borderline and narcissistic patients exceed the tolerance of group members and leaders. He views the collective demands of such patients as overwhelming and discouraging, resulting in intense countertransference reactions.

> There is little doubt that primitive feelings emerge with great rapidity and intensity in homogeneous groups of narcissis-

tic borderline patients; however, a rapid turnover with poor treatment results is the consequence. In essence, homogeneous groups of borderline or narcissistic patients lack altruism, interpersonal learning, therapeutic alliance and hope; they possess an excess of universality, ventilation, and abreaction with little group cohesion. [pp. 142–143]

On the other hand, Slavinsky-Holly (1983) has been a consistent proponent of the opposite view. She describes the benefits of being able to make group interpretations regarding characteristic borderline defenses that will apply to all participants as a means of fostering group cohesion. In addition, she advocates for homogeneous groups as a modality that allows for primitive affects to reach intense levels, which provides greater opportunity for therapist interpretation of denial, projective identification, and primitive idealization. Managing this level of intensity demands great skill (Buchele 1994) in responding to chronic problems with impulsivity, suicidal and homicidal ideation and intent, substance abuse, and acting out transference conflict, in addition to containing countertransference contempt (Klein et al. 1991).

It is difficult to take an unequivocal position regarding these two opposing views. The reader may recall studies cited earlier (Greene and Cole 1991, Leszcz et al. 1985b) that indicate borderline patients' preference for interpersonal group therapy approaches in which pathological defenses have been empathically challenged, and clarification of relationship distortions are an ongoing part of group work. The group provides realistic limits to regression when members do not permit ongoing distortions to take hold, as can happen in individual therapy because therapists are trained to allow the transference neurosis to develop. "The readier likelihood of coming out from regression makes the group meetings a safer, therapeutic environment than a dyad provides and increases the ability of reintegration, and also supports the development of intrapsychic autonomy and the laying down of psychic boundaries" (Elbirik et al. 1994, p. 148).

Borderline patients participating in mixed interpersonal inpatient groups are generally quite productive once they have stabilized through the leader's ability to display interactional balance and interpretive clarity. This manner of responding is exemplified by straightforward assertive involvement in moments of emotional intensity. This concept will be elaborated in the following section on therapeutic perspective. Borderline patients often take leadership positions in groups, even when hospitalized for as little as 24 to 48 hours, with their characteristic attempts to align with staff members as cotherapists. This fits with their intellectualized style, their ability to be insightful, and their tendency to project disowned conflict onto others.

Borderline patients display extreme sensitivity to the leader's reactions, and, when slighted, begin to disintegrate with anger, impulsivity, and the accompanying perception of the leader as the sadistic "bad object." As with the schizophrenic, the borderline tests the leader's empathic range, and group cohesion will either be fostered or diminished. If managed successfully, group members will gain understanding of how easily the narcissistic bubble, within which these patients live, can burst, resulting in frightening internal fragmentation that cannot be managed without the skill of the group leader. In a matter of minutes, the borderline cotherapist becomes a devastated, regressed individual on the verge of an explosion. Fellow patients begin to recognize the need for defensive externalization and will eventually follow up on the leader's manner of identifying precipitants within group interactions that have led to this characteristic protective posture. It is often a stabilized borderline patient who provides the self-object (Kohut 1977) function for a regressed counterpart. Once this has become the group norm, regression and resultant impulsivity can be managed by the group as a whole, rather than by the leader exclusively.

To tolerate and facilitate these intense interactions the group leader must respond empathically and without sadistic intent to the onslaught of projected criticism. These interactions challenge the therapist's character structure and often reveal unresolved narcissistic wounds through the therapist's misinterpretation of projected aggression. It has recently been noted that psychologists are not prepared to cope with the anger they encounter in their patients and themselves (Kirman 1995). I believe this dynamic often determines the success or failure of therapy for character-disordered patients.

With regard to the controversy over homogeneous vs. heterogeneous grouping of borderline and narcissistic disorders, the objectives outlined by Slavinsky-Holly (1988) can be realized in a mixed inpatient group that is functioning optimally. It is unlikely, with current managed care requirements, that homogeneous groups of patients with short hospitalizations can be effective or practical. Intensity and regression would increase and the group leader's level of skill would have to be quite high. Encouraging this level of uncovering would hardly be advisable in two to five days.

In terms of outpatient treatment, the model used at MetroWest Medical Center with greatest success combines individual and group treatment with the same psychotherapist for individuals with pronounced personality disorders. Borderline patients, for example, are added to an ongoing group of individuals with narcissistic vulnerability, but they possess a stable capacity for self–other differentiation and show less potential for regression than the characteristic borderline patient. Individual therapy is conducted until a stable therapeutic alliance has been established that will sustain individuals in the early, threatening stages of group involvement, and beyond. The established patients gain by addressing their emotional inhibition and internalization of conflict as compared to the more impulsive, acting-out individuals who gain by not being allowed to project in a chronic fashion. Rather than regress when slighted, borderline patients are encouraged to express and work through conflict with group members, an interaction that is new to them, without threat of symbiotic merger as frequently experienced in dyad relationships.

In summary, the heterogeneous group is seen as a preferred modality for both inpatient and outpatient treatment of borderline and narcissistic disorders. Homogeneous groups are seen as too regressive and difficult to manage for most psychotherapists. The one exception may be the combined individual and group model with the same psychotherapist, although this would only be conceivable on an outpatient basis and would demand very specific skills on the part of the group leader.

Adolescents

Group therapy has long been a recommended and accepted treatment for adolescents, who can show a range of disturbances. There is a large body of literature advocating and describing benefits of group treatment for adolescents. The reader is referred to Rachman and Raubolt (1984), Hurst and Gladieux (1980), and Beeferman and Orvaschel (1994).

Adolescents have traditionally been important members of inpatient heterogeneous groups. They provide unending energy that is initially met with a mixed reaction, but ultimately is often appreciated by less energetic, depressed adult and elderly patients. The young person's envy of adult authority and power has consistently been matched by adults' envy of youth and their disregard for mortality.

The opportunity for growth takes place when the adolescent expresses his or her transference, in the general sense, to adults who are experiencing significant conflict with their own adolescent daughters and sons. Distortion and misunderstanding occur at these times and lines are sometimes drawn between adults and young people. The leader's ability to monitor this conflict sensitively becomes the structure within which new understanding can be reached in an environment that is less threatening than the family. The brief inpatient group functions as the "practice field" where expression and responses are experimented with by both age groups before attempted in family therapy sessions and eventually in the home.

Homogeneous adolescent groups are useful on an outpatient basis. But the experience of the mixed group has demonstrated the benefit of adolescents having the occasions to interact with adults in a secure, structured setting.

Alcoholism

Alcoholism inpatient treatment has changed significantly in recent years with detoxification and outpatient planning being the prime focus, generally in comprehensive day programs that reduce cost and maintain efficacy. The rationale for homogeneous groupings in all settings for alcoholics and substance abusers is discussed elsewhere (Levin 1987, 1991, 1995). The area often overlooked, however, is the assessment and recognition of the varying needs of dual diagnosis and advanced recovery patients who can benefit from mixed groupings.

Inpatient programs for addictions accompanied by other disorders (depression, anxiety, personality disorder, thought disorders, etc.) are most beneficially integrated when detoxifications, psychoeducational groups, and interactional groups are also aspects of a comprehensive approach. The benefit of an interactional group is the reluctance of nonalcoholics to allow the alcoholic or addict to symbolically "take a drink" by digressing to alcoholic talk in the face of interpersonal conflict. Even more important, if there are children and spouses of alcoholics in such groups, the group recreates the alcoholic family system. As with the adolescent and adult groups, all members have an opportunity to become involved and grow in a new manner. Some of the most poignant moments in my experience have occurred when a yearning young person, plagued by an addictive family cycle, pleads with the recovering adult to explain and account for his or her abandonment of children for the bottle or the drug, accompanied by the user's longing to know what, if anything, will constitute forgiveness for his or her regretted actions.

Vannicelli and colleagues (1984) confirm the advantages of dynamic groups through their use of Yalom's (1975) interactional group therapy model:

> Many clinicians believe that alcoholic patients cannot tolerate the anxiety of an insight-oriented group. In fact, as Yalom (1975) has pointed out, even within the field of alcoholism, many who do group work expressly eschew a focus on interpersonal interaction, believing that group work with alcoholics should be limited to either a didactic focus or to the use of a supportive, suppressive, inspirational model. This is contrary to our experience over the 9 years at Appleton Treatment Center, where more than 500 patients and 60 group leaders have participated in 20 long-term interactional therapy groups. [p. 128]

On the other hand, it has been recently established, through the use of the Group Sessions Rating Scale, that groups that employ education, skill building, and less expression of emotion, and de-emphasize here-and-now interactions, are associated with fewer group members reporting drinking-related problems (Getter et al. 1992). The key variable in this study was clearly related to length of sobriety, as members began group after discharge from a twenty-one-day inpatient alcoholism program. Addiction specialists are hardly surprised by this finding as it is well known that unmodulated confrontation can unnecessarily precipitate disintegration and resultant drinking, particularly in early recovery. The value of psychoeducational groups in initial stages of treatment in the long-term acquisition of self-care skills has traditionally been undervalued in the addiction area, while successful and accepted in mental health and HIV-AIDS treatment efforts (La Salvia 1993). The results of outcome studies show the value of tailoring group type and leader persuasion to phase of treatment and diagnostic appraisal of individuals.

Inpatient dual-diagnosis programs tend to understand the necessity for an educative focus as well as having an appreciation for Kohut's (1977) understanding of the addict's self-disorder:

> The addict, finally, craves the drug because the drug seems to him to be capable of curing the central defect in his self. It becomes for him the substitute for a self-object which failed him traumatically at a time when he should still have had the feeling of omnipotently controlling its responses in accordance with his needs as if it were a part of himself. By ingesting the drug he symbolically compels the mirroring self-object to soothe him, to accept him. Or he symbolically compels the idealized self-object to submit to his merging into it and thus to his partaking in its magical power. In either case the ingestion of the drug provides him with the self-esteem which he does not possess. [p. 9]

This acknowledgment of self or personality disorder as an integral aspect of addictions does not negate or unequivocally agree with those who postulate character disorders as the cause of addictions, or conversely with those who believe addictions are the cause of character pathology (Vaillant 1983). The reality of causality is, in both camps, dependent on the uniqueness of the individual. The use of categorization interferes with the development of comprehensive treatment approaches.

Alcoholics and substance abusers initially benefit from psychoeducational group efforts designed to foster self-care and daily coping strategies and diminish threats of internal fragmentation and resultant impulsivity. Diagnostic assessments, however, are always necessary to determine personality structure and the appropriateness of parallel interactional group approaches, as in the treatment of the dual-diagnosis population. In early-stage treatment, or inpatient or day treatment, interactional methods demand skill on the part of the leader, as the addicted individual can benefit significantly from an empathic approach that facilitates the identification of emotion and the expression of perceived slights without accumulating hurts that characteristically result in "picking up." This positive experience, although brief, sets the stage for hope and outpatient planning. On the other hand, if the alcoholic's relational fear and inability to manage conflict with others is underestimated, impulsivity will result.

The outpatient interactional mixed group is an excellent adjunct to AA. As relational confidence builds in the program, the individual can, once sobriety has been solidly established, gain more expertise in identifying and working through conflict, often in a manner never previously understood. Aggression, impulsivity, sexual urges, and perceived humiliations become feeling states to be examined rather than intolerances that can only be managed through the use of substances that restore a feeble sense of self.

Eating Disorders

Individuals with a different addiction, namely eating disorders, are frequently represented on inpatient units, in the patient population of private practitioners, and in counseling centers. These patients struggle with depression, personality disorders, and anxiety reactions, and are often cross-addicted. As with the alcoholic population, diagnostic assessment is therefore critical in terms of understanding the overall function of the eating disorder. Homogeneous groups for this population serve a similar function, as with other addictions, in reducing isolation of the disturbance, reducing intolerable self-hatred, and managing intense shame in what is often perceived as a safer environment than individual therapy (Aronson 1993).

The inpatient model used at MetroWest Medical Center provides separate tracks for dual-diagnosed addiction patients and eating disorder patients, with both groups being combined with other diagnostic entities in a daily interactional groups, community meetings, and psychoeducational opportunities. The difficulty in engaging anorexic patients in group therapy has been highlighted by several authors (Hall 1985, Riese and Rutan 1992) with the frequent conclusion that these individuals are extremely sensitive to criticism, imagined or real, and characteristically avoid any recognition of unpleasant feelings through their obsessive preoccupation with food. In fact, the commonality between the alcoholic and eating-disordered patients in group is their responding to conflict by talking about food or drink.

It has been consistently observed that eating-disordered individuals long for a rescuing self-object when interpersonal conflict is in the air. Goodsitt (1985) states, "Once the therapist accepts he is dealing with a deficit in the self, he is encouraged to go beyond confrontive and interpretive interventions. Long ago, Hilde Bruch (1962) realized the futility of interpretation in working with anorexics. I propose that what is effective is the therapist's actively filling in the deficits in the patient's self. The main thrust of therapeutic activity is to manage the transference rather than to interpret it" (p. 56).

The inpatient group leader who understands the necessity of empathic self-object relating, provided that the patient's weight has been stabilized, has the opportunity to facilitate the eating-disordered patient's emotional reaction to perceived conflict in a manner that may have seldom been experienced. The mixed group, particularly with impulsive members present, can produce significant anxiety in the anorectic to the point where restricting food seems like the only viable means of coping. However, when the leader is able to sensitively guide the expression of the patient's reaction to others, a beginning pattern of assertion is fostered without the feared outcome of rejection or verbal abuse.

Some therapists may object that this recommendation is theoretically interesting but is highly unlikely to be followed, given the demands of inpatient work and leader expertise. The answer to this objection is that success is both possible and probable. What is critical to the recovery process is the therapist learning about the interactional origins of addictive behavior and the interactive responses and skills that remedy early relational disappointments and build the sense of self.

Bulimic patients have generally been more able to work in mixed inpatient groups than anorexics, and some believe a heterogeneous group is more therapeutic than a homogeneous group for inpatients (Lacey 1985). The Center for the Study of Anorexia and Bulimia (1984) states: "Most of the bulimic people we see are terribly isolated and are often unable to take part in ordinary social activities, even if they maintain successful work lives. Other group members are frequently the first people in each other's lives to know about the problem. The group is the first place the bulimic can relax and be herself. Coming out of 'hiding' with the help of the group is a major step toward self-acceptance and is an enormous relief" (p. 2).

Homogeneous groups for eating disorders are recommended in inpatient, day treatment, and outpatient programs. The mixed inpatient group is ineffective with anorexics unless body weight has been regulated and other treatment modalities (i.e., individual, family) have been established. When these criteria have been met, there is a significant opportunity for outpatient work. Bulimic patients who can discuss their problem are productive in mixed groups. Their dynamics are often perceived as more understandable to non–eating-disordered patients than to restricters, who restrict food intake exclusively rather than bingeing and purging.

Mixed outpatient groups should also be considered when eating is clearly stabilized and relational issues continue to be significant impediments to quality of life. Short-term cognitive group approaches have proven to be effective (Brownell and Foreyt 1986, Mitchell et al. 1993) but open-ended psychodynamic groups can also be extremely effective in reducing hospital admissions and providing interpersonal interactions that lessen the drive to communicate indirectly and covertly (Riese and Rutan 1992).

Affective Disorders

Homogeneous group therapy has been recommended for those suffering from major affective disorders and PTSD, and for the depressed elderly. Some theorists (e.g., Yalom

1975) have found that the inclusion of manic-depressives in mixed groups is inappropriate. It has been typical of the inpatient milieu to exclude manic individuals from the stimulation of the group as their presence is obviously overwhelming and counterproductive for all involved. Once medication management has effected stabilization, patients are generally encouraged to participate in group programs, and their inclusion is often very encouraging to other patients who have observed the change in the bipolar patient from admission to group participation. This dramatic change tends to decrease fears of medication for the other patients as well as stimulate hope of recovery.

The bipolar patient's inclusion in a group usually results in one of two reactions: (1) they deny any interpersonal difficulties and view their hospitalization as solely for the need to reestablish lithium treatment; (2) they acknowledge the depth of their depression and interact like severely depressed patients. The first type of patient is more easily engaged if other patients are also receiving lithium. Interactions are similar to those described in outpatient manic-depression groups:

> Increased interest in lithium maintenance and its risks and benefits often seemed to serve as the focus of the member's interest during this period and seemed to indicate the integration of the patient in the group. The new member was often surprised to discover that other members were the source of a great deal of information about lithium use;

other group members provided support and reassurance to the new member during this period. The new member would begin to show more interest in his own treatment, e.g., inquiring about blood levels, describing its various side effects, etc. The common interest in lithium served to foster cohesiveness in the group. Other common themes included the patient's considerable skepticism about lithium treatment and the patient's sense of loss of the periods of mild-to-moderate euphoria he is less likely to experience when maintained on lithium. Members often found that they were forced to make changes in their work and social habits as a result of the loss of these periods. [Volmar et al. 1981, p. 230]

Based on their research and review of the literature, the authors found that homogeneous group psychotherapy as an adjunct to lithium prophylaxis can significantly reduce hospitalizations. Their long-term psychotherapy groups reduced hospital days by nearly 75 percent, although they emphasize that the pronounced interpersonal difficulties of these patients demands intense work as their relational problems can consistently jeopardize lithium management. A summary of the literature (Kanas 1993) further supports these findings and additionally emphasizes that several group researchers working exclusively with bipolar populations report similar ratings of curative factors to Yalom's outpatient groups for neurotic patients.

The inpatient mixed group has typically been a forum

for discussion of medications and their effects, particularly as patients discuss their emotional difficulty in accepting the need for external agents. Ultimately, though, as the alcoholic and eating-disordered patients are asked not to digress to food or drink talk in the face of interpersonal conflict, so the manic-depressive is requested to address relational issues, rather than solely discussing medications. Some patients consistently resist this request, while the majority will join in with other group members of varying diagnoses who talk of their ongoing sense of depression. It has been estimated that depression is part of the clinical picture of nearly every inpatient (Betcher 1983) and this acknowledgment allows the individual suffering from manic-depression, as well as others, to foster group cohesiveness through establishing a common ground of distress. This potentially provides the foundation from which the interpersonal aspects of depression can be explored.

Group psychotherapy exclusive to bipolar disturbances and mixed groups are both recommended in inpatient and day treatment programs, while the literature has clearly established the efficacy of homogeneous groups for this population on an outpatient basis. The exceptions to this guideline are individuals who do not suffer manic episodes and are not prone to psychotic states, but rather experience pronounced depressions with clear interactional precipitants.

Loss and depression, as all clinicians realize, are intimately linked, but no more so than among the elderly.

Cooper (1981), in an award-winning paper, highlights the consensus view that Freud's pessimism regarding psycho-analytic work with those over 50 has been unfounded. He cites group therapy as being especially effective with the elderly:

> The multiple losses of the elderly tend to create a shrink-ing of their world of relationships. Due to their own dimin-ishing physical, or mental, or both, capacities and to changes in the external world, such as the withdrawal of support through death or social rejection, aging is often equated with increasing isolation. While internal conflicts and the construction of meanings are as important to at-tend to in the therapy of the elderly as in that of any age group, group psychotherapy combines this therapeutic attention with socialization opportunities and thereby pre-sents a high order of specificity in refurbishing the supplies needed by the deprived, rejected, and regressed elderly pa-tient. [p. 205]

The mixed inpatient group is often enriched by the presence of elderly patients, as they sometimes serve in the role of grandparent mediator of conflict between ado-lescent and middle-aged adults. At times, it is as if one is witnessing generational transferences, and this has pro-vided an opportunity for self-expansion while adding a real-world element to the group experience. It is notewor-thy how often adolescent and elderly patients befriend each other in short hospital stays.

The elderly patient's continual focus on loss has also facilitated the expression of sad affect from depressed individuals of all ages. Additionally, defensive responses to the elderly's concentration on loss reveals precipitants to masked depression, as well as revealing group members' tolerance for sad affect, which enhances interpersonal diagnostic assessments.

It has been pointed out that therapists working with the elderly must be aware of the dual transference of therapist-as-parent and therapist-as-child (Johnson et al. 1985).

> Parent and child have traded places out of necessity, yet this reversal of the relationship is often a highly ambivalent one, entailing some embarrassment and resentment of the children. The therapist becomes both the object of idealization as the magical replacement of the loving and dependable parent, and at the same time, the resented child who has usurped the parental role. . . . These two basic transference positions often conflict. Expression of the envy or resentment toward the therapist-as-child might threaten the image of the therapist-as-parent, so these feelings are often repressed or more often displaced onto nursing staff or other patients. [p. 120]

The elderly have come to be viewed as a group that can respond to psychotherapeutic work, particularly homogeneous group therapy (Berland and Poggi 1979, Clark and Vorst 1994, Zerhusen et al. 1991). These authors estimate that depression among those over 65 affects 50 percent of the population, while others contend that elderly narcissistic injuries demand the greatest need for validating and self-affirming self-objects than any other time in the life cycle (Leszcz et al. 1985a). The National Institutes of Health (1991) also confirm the high incidence of depression in the elderly, and report that this population is treated infrequently compared with younger individuals. Additionally, their data indicate the effectiveness of combining antidepressant medication with group psychotherapy, which is their recommended protocol for treatment of elderly depression.

Group psychotherapy is unquestionably recommended for the depressed elderly, with both mixed and homogeneous groups in inpatient settings being useful. Outpatient groups, however, are seen as most effective with age and diagnostic matching.

Childhood Abuse

The high prevalence of depression in the elderly is also matched by the estimates of childhood abuse in the psychiatric population overall. The estimates of several researchers regarding this correlation range from 36 to 70 percent (Zaidi 1994) with estimates of rape and domestic violence in the general population being as high as 25 to 33 percent (Herman 1992). The inpatient group leader must be extremely sensitive to PTSD as exploration and interpretation without careful assessment of each individual's capacity to tolerate the intense emotion associated with remembering can be quite regressive and can constitute the repetition of a trauma that cannot be adequately managed in a brief hospital stay.

Providing uncovering or supportive interventions is critical to facilitating trust in a population that has been robbed of human dignity. Individual therapy is often the initial treatment of choice until trust and safety can be established, with the homogeneous group being essential to the beginning process of regaining trust in others. Group approaches, especially when hospitalization has been necessary, are less threatening when psychoeducative and cognitive in nature. Allen and Bloom (1994) summarize guidelines used in determining whether avoidance or approach techniques are best suited to the trauma victim:

> Supportive approaches are indicated when traumatic memories are intrusive and an individual's self-capacities to master or cope with distressing affect are limited. Uncovering approaches may be useful when a person's resources are able to cope with affect, and self-capacities are strong enough to allow increased awareness or recall of traumatic experiences. In a survey of 18 psychologists nationally prominent for their use of flooding or implosive (approach) techniques, it was found that these exposure treatments were used in only 58% of the PTSD cases treated by them. Exposure tech-

niques were contraindicated by marked psychological dysfunction, personality disorder, suicidality, impulsiveness, substance abuse, or treatment resistance. [p. 428]

Inpatient psychoeducative efforts have been effective with PTSD victims when initially homogeneous and educative in nature, with possible inclusion in mixed groups depending on personality variables and proximity to traumatic events. It has, in fact, been recommended that involvement in time-limited homogeneous groups be followed by group therapy with diverse diagnosis so as to prevent collective victim identity united against a cruel world in a regressive manner. An additional fear is manifested when such a group is led by an idealized leader invested in protecting members from further harm (van der Kolk 1987). It is critical for the long-term benefit of the abused to be able to relate to their milieu as a whole rather than being convinced that safety only exists with those similarly abused, as this narrow perspective ultimately contributes to entrenched fears of involvement with the world at large. Judith Herman, in her classic text *Trauma and Recovery* (1992), cites several examples of group therapy surpassing the effectiveness of individual therapy through the group's collective ability to bear and integrate traumatic experience beyond the capacity of any individual member. She additionally comments on group formation according to stage of recovery:

Some of the bewildering variability in groups begins to make sense when matched to the therapeutic tasks of the three major stages of recovery. First-stage groups concern themselves primarily with the task of establishing safety. They focus on basic self-care, one day at a time. Second-stage groups concern themselves primarily with the traumatic event. They focus on coming to terms with the past. Third-stage groups concern themselves primarily with re-integrating the survivor into the community of ordinary people. They focus on interpersonal relationships in the present. The structure of each type of group is adapted to its primary task. [p. 217]

We have now reached the end of the section on group composition for various diagnostic entities, with the author's clear awareness that descriptive diagnosis has been used for convenience rather than comprehensively describing the uniqueness of any individual. The next section addresses the theoretical orientation of the group therapist, and discusses the use of self-psychology, object relations, and psychoeducative concepts.

THERAPEUTIC PERSPECTIVE: INSIGHT (PSYCHODYNAMIC) VERSUS SUPPORTIVE (EDUCATIVE) PSYCHOTHERAPY

The literature has suggested guidelines for group composition based on diagnosis. It has also advocated the inclusion of object relations, self-psychology, and psycho-educative methods in group treatment. The modifications of classical analytic thought by object relations and self-psychology theorists has been viewed as a parallel development of culture and theory (Klein et al. 1992), accepting the primacy of relationships in the emotional problems psychotherapists are presented with today. This section samples each modality through excerpts from the literature (Table 3–1).

The International Journal of Group Psychotherapy contrasted two views as represented by Russakoff and Oldham (1984), who advocated an insight-oriented object relations approach to inpatient group therapy, and Maxmen (1984), who espoused a nonpsychoanalytic alternative called an educative group model, created specifically for treating short-term inpatients.

Table 3–1. Stages of Group Psychotherapy

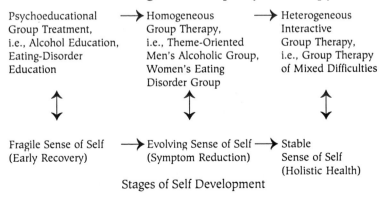

Psychoeducational Group Treatment, i.e., Alcohol Education, Eating-Disorder Education	→	Homogeneous Group Therapy, i.e., Theme-Oriented Men's Alcoholic Group, Women's Eating Disorder Group	→	Heterogeneous Interactive Group Therapy, i.e., Group Therapy of Mixed Difficulties
↕		↕		↕
Fragile Sense of Self (Early Recovery)	→	Evolving Sense of Self (Symptom Reduction)	→	Stable Sense of Self (Holistic Health)

Stages of Self Development

Object relations theory is discussed in detail elsewhere (Horner 1979, 1990, Kernberg 1975, 1976, Klein et al. 1992). Russakoff and Oldham, who were supervised by Otto Kernberg, believe it to be critical to understand the

concepts of internalized self and object representations. . . . Two versions of such internalization processes are the positive or libidinally linked part-self and part-object representations, and the negative, or aggressively linked part-self and part-object representation. Recognition of this point is of crucial importance, as is a fact that these processes coexist in a mutually contradictory way in many hospitalized patients. . . . The part aspect of these conceptualizations indicates that at any given time, a patient's view of himself or of others is typically distorted by primitive mental processes, such as splitting, denied aspects of himself, projection of hostile impulses onto others, and so on. [pp. 341–342]

The authors believe that previous psychoanalytic work with inpatients has failed because it has been determined by a simplified model that focuses on pure affects and drives without being linked to self and object representations. This focusing on feelings in isolation is viewed as counterproductive with borderline and psychotic patients in particular. The authors seem to be emphasizing therapists' inclination to help patients label feelings while losing focus on how internal and external perceptions determine affective states.

The above simplified theoretical example can now be complemented by Russakoff and Oldham's recommended technique:

> The therapist must first clarify within the group the elements that constitute the fundamental units of the object relations conflict. Second, the therapist must confront the patient with the presence of these units. Sometimes—more often in borderline patients—the act of confronting the patient helps the patient organize his thinking more realistically, and to integrate his part-self and part-object representation. When such an interpretation does not have as helpful an impact as the therapist would expect, fuller interpretation of both sides of the conflict-introject and project is indicated. [p. 350]

Primitively disturbed individuals react to correct interpretations with silence followed by more integrated functioning or by rageful reactions. These interpretations are described as lengthy and contrary to traditional training that emphasized short statements to highly disturbed individuals, as it is believed that the unique nature of object relations concepts allows for an expressive approach, even with the very disturbed being treated on short-term units.

Maxmen (1984), on the other hand, created an educative model based partly on his original research (1973), in which inpatients ranked installation of hope, group cohesiveness, altruism, and universality as the most helpful factors in group therapy. He describes his modality as atheoretical in that the etiology of mental illness is assumed to be unknown, thus regarding mental illness as akin to medical illness with symptoms viewed as independent of one's personality. Maxmen explains that his modality is not aimed at alternating symptoms, but its objective is to help patients cope with their illness. He cautions against setting unrealistic expectations that cannot be realized by hospitalized patients, only reinforcing feelings of inadequacy. He states:

> An educative model is often accused of being superficial, or of lacking an appreciation of psychodynamic complexities, or of being simple-minded. Perhaps these are valid comments. But complexity is not virtue; yet neither is simplicity. . . . Pragmatic, not theoretical, considerations should dictate treatment. It is hoped that patients can survive theories. Groups should help, and this objective, though not pretentious, should be examined repeatedly and not lost amid ideological preoccupations. [p. 367]

The object relations and educative models cited above do appear to be opposites, with one emphasizing interpretation and the other instructive living. Several structured cognitive group approaches treating early phases of alcohol, substance abuse, eating disorders, and postpartum depression have recently rendered successful outcomes and are most akin to the educative-instructional persuasion (Getter et al. 1992, Greun 1993, LaSalvia 1993, Mitchell et al. 1993). Successful outcomes have also been found for significant personality disorders using interactional models akin to Yalom's with integration of object relations techniques, even in initial phases of treatment (Buchele 1994, Greene and Cole 1991, Klein et al. 1991, Tschuschke and Dies 1994).

One interesting alternative to the interpretive-instructive debate, with the above outcome findings in mind, is the implementation of graded group programs to address varying levels of disturbance from admission to discharge, to day treatment, to outpatient treatment (Betcher et al. 1982, Leopold 1976, Leszcz et al. 1985b). Leopold developed a total treatment program for hospitalized patients involving three levels specifically designed for varying emotional and behavioral capabilities. Groups were designed from structured and supportive for most regressed patients, to a second level with increased focus on intermember relationships, to the highest level group composed of outpatients and patients nearing discharge where interpersonal conflicts within the group were utilized as learning opportunities.

The graded treatment approaches are "middle of the road" in comparison to the two models initially cited. Betcher (1983), in his discussion on "premises of the leader," accurately represents the therapeutic stance advocated by the intermediate position. He advocates leaders developing group cohesion through reliance on the premise that it is the alternation in relationships between members that carries the most potential for growth. Additionally, active problem solving is encouraged among members rather than with the leader exclusively. The leader is expected to maintain boundaries through confidentiality within the group and by making a strong effort to keep all members in the room for the entire session, even if this necessitates allowing agitated patients to pace in the corner. Firm boundaries, believed to convey tolerance for close proximity to others and tolerance of intense affect, are set by the leader. He further encourages emphasis on intermember relating with active intervention if long silences occur, as they are viewed as aversive to inpatients.

He further encourages the leader to arbitrate interpersonal conflict, to foster inclusion of all members, and to focus interventions on intermember relationships rather than exploring historical material and making deep interpretations of transference reactions, as this technique is viewed as too regressive and not contributing to group cohesion.

Hannah (1984), in two insightful papers, also maintains an intermediate position regarding the two approaches cited. However, because she conceptualizes, from an object relations point of view, her remarks are of a different nature than those advocating a graded treatment approach.

My position is most similar to Hannah's median approach in technique, although we employ different theoretical constructs to understand experience. She comments:

> The questions I raise about Russakoff and Oldham's article concern my sense that their interventions, although theoretically correct, are at times too far removed from the immediate experience of the patients in the group, whereas my questions about Maxmen's approach suggest that important latent aspects of the patient's communications, having to do with underlying conflicts and group dynamics, may be overlooked if the pragmatics of getting along in the world are the major focus of the therapist's remarks. [1984, p. 370]

This critique is believed to be accurate; the only point of contention is whether or not the object relations viewpoint is "theoretically correct." For instance, Hannah (1984) questions whether

> integration of split-off self-and-object representations can be accomplished in a brief hospital stay. Although I can agree that there is progress in the ability of the group to express meaningful feelings, I would question whether this was because of the theoretical accuracy of the lengthy interpretations. My own explanations would point to a process occurring in the group wherein the therapist was perceived as actively attempting to understand and to clarify

the feelings of the members of the group, with empathy and a tolerance for, or containment of, the disturbing aggressive elements in the room. [p. 371]

Having been influenced by the object relations theory of Kernberg (1975, 1976, 1980) and particularly Horner (1979, 1990), I agree with Hannah that such interventions are overly long and quite ambitious. In addition, the object relations clinician uses the familiar defenses of projection and, particularly, projective identification to solely account for the character-disordered individual's reactions, without acknowledging that a perception of the psychotherapist begins this reactive cycle. This perception may be a distortion or it may be exemplary of the patient's ability to sense a vulnerability in others, such as the therapist being tired or preoccupied. The intent of the patient's observation may be to unleash a sadistic impulse, or frequently it is an attempt to care for the therapist as the patient has for a vulnerable parent. Whatever the historical origin and current intent may be, it is enormously frustrating for the patient if the reaction is viewed as simply a historical repetition rather than having perceptual validity in the present. It is wrong to assume that disturbed patients project their internal conflict similarly to all psychotherapists; we all engender different sequences of transference and non-transference material based on our reactive capacities, particularly in the all-important area of aggression. It is hardly ever the projected aggression of the patient that determines the fate of psychotherapy. It is, however, quite likely that the aggression of the therapist will be a major determinant of the treatment outcome. This point is extremely important in terms of group therapy as the members are watching the therapist manage his or her own aggressive impulses, often in relation to the character-disordered individual, as the therapist then displays his or her ability to repeat trauma or understand its interactional origins through exemplary interactional responses.

Several years ago, attempting to explore the interactional benefits of object relations therapy, I made interpretations of length akin to the technical style advocated by Russakoff and Oldham. They received favorable responses from the patients. I then asked patients in subsequent sessions what they understood me to be conveying to them. It became clear that the patients had little understanding of such comments, but nevertheless felt comforted by my interest in them. Insight was not forthcoming but group cohesion was developed, one exception being in terms of patient understanding when comments were concisely made regarding the nature of ambivalence and the use of splitting mechanisms. Hannah (1984) maintains that patients, "require hospitalization when the splitting mechanism fails and the 'good' self-and-object representations are overrun by aggression; self-object differentiation may then break down, possibly as a last resort to ward off total destruction" (p. 260).

Hannah's understanding of why lengthy object relations interpretations seem to be perceived positively, and why the failure of the defense of splitting seems to precipitate hospitalization, can be viewed from a self-psychology perspective also. Heeding Maxmen's advice that "groups do not exist to test etiological speculations," the basic differences in the nature of man seen from object relations and self-psychology points of view will not be examined here. The reader is referred to Kohut (1984), Chessick (1985), White and Weiner (1986), Rowe and Mac Isaac (1991).

The positive reaction to the detailed object relations interpretations is likely a product of the soothing tension-regulating function of a therapeutic self–self-object relationship. We now begin to shift from the narrow debate of insight versus support or education to the idea that possibly what preoedipal-disordered patients need most are self-objects who are empathically attuned and able to respond, without undue bias, to the internal world of the individual.

A brief digression is necessary to clarify the intended meaning of self–self-object relating and the intended meaning of the term *empathy*. Self-objects are experienced as part of the self. "If optimally experienced during childhood [they] remain one of the pillars of mental health throughout life and, in the reverse, if the self-objects of childhood fail, then the resulting psychological deficits or distortions will remain a burden that will have to be carried throughout life" (Kohut 1977, pp. 87–88).

The term *self-object* is used in this instance to connote "that dimension of our experience of another person that relates to this person's functions in shoring up the self" (Kohut 1974, p. 44). *Empathy*, on the other hand, is defined as the ability to understand and respond to the inner world of another with the intent of fostering progressive personal development. This definition differs slightly in intent from Kohut's classic definition of empathy as vicarious introspection. He emphasized the ability to understand the inner world of another as an observational tool that could be utilized constructively or destructively. Kohut used Hitler's understanding of the German people prior to World War II as an example of the destructive use of empathy. The revised definition, in this context, emphasizes the positive use of empathy to foster the personal growth of another.

The type of relating described by the self–self-object construct leads to management of primitive anxiety within a relationship, and thus fosters the patient's hope that troubling tension can be shared and managed nondestructively. The ultimate long-term gain of this process is in the creation of new inner structure, a new capability to keep one's self intact under significant internal and external duress. The immediate gain is the reestablishment of self-cohesion, which has been fragmented due to per-

ceived failures of self-objects outside the hospital or treatment center. Rather than focusing on the interpretation
of failure of defenses (splitting), this gain is viewed as a
by-product and thus secondary to understanding disturbances in self–self-object relationships. The management
of a damaged self through the process of internalization,
the taking in of another's ability to self-regulate tension
through participation in quality interactions where the
psychotherapist displays interactional balance, is a manner of responding to another that exemplifies neither
the extreme of aggression nor submission, but rather
straightforward assertive involvement in moments of emotional intensity. This ability of the psychotherapist allows
the patient to observe and internalize the integration of
thought, emotion, and expression that is not primarily
based on historic underpinnings or stereotypical role
adherence. That is to say, the psychotherapist's reactive
manner is mostly balanced in terms of clarity of perception, not predicated upon prior unresolved conflict
or fixed sex-role definition. Patients whose sense of
self has suffered from the extremes of either parental
emotional onslaughts or parental detachment, or both,
have little experience with a state of being at ease with
themselves, and they have little experience with tolerance
of a mix of feeling toward self or other without fragmentation of relationship or oneself. Therefore, the interactional
balance of the psychotherapist, and ultimately the patient,

becomes a critical component of recovery. A developmental example of this process is a parent's attempt to soothe an anxious child, which, when managed reasonably many times, results in the child's own internal voice being self-understanding rather than punitive or permissive, and in equitable assessments of self and others.

How can such relational criteria be established in a very brief hospital stay, or in an outpatient setting under the umbrella of managed care guidelines? These interactional criteria are viewed as relevant to each relational opportunity, as each therapeutic response builds part of the foundation necessary for internal continuity and cohesion. The psychotherapist or milieu clinician must believe that his or her manner of responsiveness, from the tone of saying "good morning," to supportive and interpretive comments are of high value and necessary to initiate the patient's complex and often long road to developing a balanced sense of self. Interactions, although brief, may be negatively or positively influential. Brief does not mean insignificant and, in fact, such quality interactions are often the reason the patient stays in treatment.

We could be sidetracked into a debate often initiated by self psychologists about what is the curative agent: insight or transmuting internalizations leading to structural transformation. This focus is far too narrow and polarizing when in reality the combined relational methods of object relations, with its emphasis on the identification of the defenses of projection, projective identification, splitting, and primitive denial, can be complemented by the understanding of relational sequences and by the responsiveness of the self psychologist. Defenses are thus understood in the context of relational perceptions rather than as character flaws identified in isolation, giving the patient clear understanding of the perceptual patterns that result in the believed necessity of defense.

From this perspective the psychotherapist is now in the optimal listening position to provide the five necessary elements for positive change: empathy, interactional balance, tension management, internalization, and interpretation. Each is a separate ability of the therapist, although interconnected and interdependent. Interpretations, for instance, are difficult to accept and internalize without the patient's tension being modulated through the empathy and balance of the psychotherapist.

The authors cited in this section are representative of theoretical positions highlighted. However, object relations and self psychology are modalities initially designed for individual analysis, are still being adapted to group work, and thus are likely to be practiced somewhat differently, depending on the group leader's personality and theory. Cognitive therapists also differ from Maxmen's narrow theoretical persuasion in that cognitive outcome studies have demonstrated more expansive gains, and conceptually more ambitious gains are expected.

SUMMARY

This chapter reviewed the group outcome literature and the complexities of group composition and therapeutic orientation. Characteristic biases regarding group treatment have been discussed. Group treatment is a primary modality that is very much in tune with rapid societal change. This unprecedented rate of change, with its accompanying sense of alienation and estrangement from relational intimacy, has stressed the healthiest individuals and their family lives, while leaving the most vulnerable in a state of fragmentation.

Those of us committed to understanding the interplay between cultural movement and the individual have been attempting to identify the relational ingredients that lead some to adapt to change, as compared to those who seem to fall apart in the face of perceived newness and dissimilarity.

It is imperative, in this age of cost containment and accountability, that the psychotherapist identify and describe the therapeutic elements that constitute healing for specific disturbances. Group psychotherapy plays a critical role in helping individuals with a range of capabilities cope and adapt to relational and societal change. Refined selection criteria determine the choice of group modality. It is likely that individuals will move from homogeneous, psychoeducational experiences to mixed psychotherapy groups where diversity and dissimilarity are initially tolerated and ultimately welcomed. The individual's world, internally and externally, broadens, and new members are seen as bringing new energy and new perspective. The interplay between diversity and universal human longings is recognized, as the need for merging with perceived perfection of others has lessened. Internal structure has accumulated as a result of many quality interactions of intensity and balance; thus the threat of disintegration has been markedly reduced and the world can be experienced as an opportunity for self-expansion, rather than as a chronic opportunity for repeated defeat and humiliation.

I frequently experience the old cliché "we are all more alike than different" in mixed outpatient groups, particularly as new members are added and often feel they do not fit with "these types of people." It has been immensely uplifting to observe and participate as exterior personas melt, maladaptive defenses are put aside, and the uniqueness and similarities of the individuals are revealed. This occurrence never comes easily, but always after many arduous interactions. It is reminiscent of being taught or teaching someone to ride a bike for the first time. We, the facilitators, are fortunate, for we are assured of getting another swing of the bat, another chance to sing the favorite song and rewrite our history as we pass on our new refined ability. Let's all give those who give us this ongoing opportunity the same chance!

❧ 4 ❧

Broken Hearts Mending on the Path to Holism: Five Case Studies

This chapter gives concrete examples of how a unique psychotherapeutic model of combined individual and group psychotherapy is ideally suited to treat abuse and addiction sufferers. This model is cost-effective, it prevents and eliminates the need for hospitalization, and, most important, it stabilizes patients' sense of self so that the health habits of alternative medicine support can be used.

This model emphasizes individual therapy as the key stabilizer that provides the bridge to successful group psychotherapy. Individual therapy is the initial step to building a therapeutic alliance with individuals who have a fragile sense of self and who suffered abuse and addiction. This alliance allows individuals to tolerate the intensity of group interactions without internal fragmentation.

Once the psychotherapist is trusted and viewed as one whose empathy provides understanding and compassion, individuals can participate in an intensive group.

Groups are intensive in that they emphasize an in-depth study of interactions as clues to origins of difficulties, as well as in-depth study of constructive means of interacting. Participants are asked to limit contact with each other outside of group sessions, with confidentiality being of paramount importance. Interactional balance, as described in the previous chapter, is the ability of the therapist to facilitate change and provide empathy, tension management, and the opportunity for internalization and interpretation. In this model, interpretations of abuse of self and others are not based on the belief that these behaviors are innate, but rather that they are learned relationally and unlearned relationally.

Five case studies are presented in which abuse and addiction played a part. I provide a brief history of each individual and relevant aspects of their early individual sessions. I emphasize group interactions that resulted in the most growth and change.

PAT

Pat is a middle-aged professional woman who requested individual psychotherapy after two extended-family members died within six months of each other. She also revealed that loss had precipitated depression for her in the past, citing that her very accomplished father had committed suicide when she was a young girl and both her siblings had attempted suicide at one time in their lives. Her ex-husband was an active alcoholic and she drank daily "to kill the pain" until she joined Al-Anon at a friend's insistence. Recently her psychotherapist of many years had moved and she found herself depressed again without the support she had counted on. The previous psychotherapy was described as friendly and supportive; sessions were scheduled when needed, usually twice a month.

Pat had tried valiantly to raise her adult children in a loving, informed way. She related in a cautious manner, although making clear that she was in dire need of help. It was quite apparent that although she invested much faith in my position of authority ("You're the doctor"), she also manifested a great deal of fear in her worry about rejection. This theme of longing for closeness with and assurance from males, while expecting repeated abandonment, then became the core of her treatment. The initial phase of individual therapy consisted of examining her abandonment perceptions, without reaffirming her greatest fear: "I'm abnormal." Her fear of repeating the depression of her father and siblings was enormous, and her relationship with her egocentric mother provided no hope for a different outcome. She saw her mother deteriorate after her father's death, living an isolated life devoid of human connection. Her additional fear was that she would someday risk involvement with another man to discover that she made a poor choice, another alcoholic or depressed man who would be unavailable and ultimately abandon her. Pat smoked two packs of cigarettes a day, consumed a poor diet, and did not exercise, meditate, or take care of her health. She used Valium to soothe herself. This was changed to an antidepressant after trust was established and she was willing to make the change.

Pat's depression lessened as weekly individual sessions focused on providing her with an in-depth understanding of the sequential thought and feeling patterns that led her to perceptions of abandonment and rejection from the past. Her perceptions of her therapist were most critical and were examined in a manner that did not reinforce her being abnormal for having such ideas, but rather established that all perceptions are understandable if we have knowledge of their origin. Distortions would be corrected with this foundation in mind, giving credibility to her perceptions because they were understandable in light of the experiences she had endured. In addition, the reality aspect of her perceptions needed to be differentiated. For example, she would comment that I looked tired during sessions preceding my vacation. On occasion, she would comment that maybe the work had worn me down; inevitably this would lead to the fear that I was sick of her and would not return or, even worse, that she had driven me to illness. Pat had had several dreams in which

I would become terminally ill or die in an accident. Her fear of abandonment as pertains to her father's suicide was immense. Her growing attachment bred fears of loss, as her dreams reflected the earlier trauma. The reality perception of tiredness became fertile ground for historical material to emerge. It became necessary to convey again to Pat that these concerns were understandable, given her life experiences. The empathy and interactional balance displayed as these interpretations were made provided Pat an opportunity to internalize an understanding self-voice, rather than the punitive voice she had been utilizing for years. She began to learn that we form our internal voice through many interactions with others, which then leads to our ability to assess our actions and reactions. If our internal voice is extreme, we then must learn to monitor these extremes through internalizing the voice of more reasonable, reality-based individuals in our lives, individuals who neither placate us nor criticize unjustly.

MARK

Mark is a middle-aged married man, and the father of three adult children. He requested individual treatment after one year of recovery from alcoholism. His alcohol counselor felt at this time that his depression and aggressive behavior needed more intensive work. Mark had attended AA meetings regularly since a brief detox admission and had an AA sponsor whom he talked with weekly.

Nevertheless, he felt his social relationships still remained quite poor.

Mark, the older of two siblings, described his mother as self-centered and manipulative, while his relationship with his deceased father had been estranged, although he had held him in high esteem. He particularly respected his father's work ethic, which he described as excessive, but he nevertheless identified strongly with his father as he defined himself almost exclusively through his work experiences. It was quite clear that he seriously doubted his relational abilities. It was also clear that his aggressive work style masked a great deal of self-doubt, guilt, and perceived inadequacy. Mark saw his addiction counselor when needed, averaging sessions once every two or three weeks.

Mark expressed aggression forcefully to others and in fact had been in several shouting matches with his employees as he began treatment. Although Pat internalized aggression, she and Mark had similar internal voices of punitiveness, disapproval and, at times, self-hatred. Abuse of self and others is a protective, learned mechanism that is used to guard a fragile sense of self. The degree of Mark's self-hatred necessitated antidepressant medications. In the initial months he brought himself to the emergency room requesting hospitalization for suicidal thoughts and was admitted for a brief period.

Pat's core sensitivity emerged as her fear of abandonment, "You'll leave me if I get close." Mark's core sensitivity, however, emerged as, "You'll humiliate me if I get close." His reactiveness, we learned, was predicated upon a perception of being thought incapable, of less capable than his internal ideal for himself. He came out fighting when he thought people were confirming his worst fears of incompetence. He consistently overreacted and used alcohol to appease his grandiosity and soothe his anxiety and impulsiveness. He talked of "making things happen" in business and "rising to the occasion" when the pressure was on and something exceptional was required for success. He attributed his drive and ability to function with little sleep to alcohol. Alcohol was clearly used as an extension of self to reinforce his desire for perfection; it was simply described as an effective means of doing business and fending off feelings of inadequacy. In fact, my initial interpretation of Mark's aggression as a futile attempt to protect himself from being humiliated puzzled and angered him at the same time. His anger toward me became the cornerstone of our work, as this process revealed the sequences of his thinking that resulted in impulsivity. We carefully explored his reactiveness, not only in therapy but with others in his daily life as well. He began to understand that vulnerability was not synonymous with humiliation. He saw a male authority, whom he came to respect, attempt earnestly to understand the nature of his reactions rather than as someone preoccupied with capitalizing on his errors to elevate himself. The interpersonal balance of the therapist again became the key to Mark's internalizing a more understanding view of himself, rather than returning to punitive self-assessments that fueled his self-hatred.

Mark also suffered from poor nutrition, high cholesterol, and high blood pressure. He had formerly exercised, but abandoned this several years ago and was now 25 pounds overweight. I questioned him about characteristic nutritional patterns because I thought that he was likely hypoglycemic, as his behavior was consistent with erratic blood sugar levels.

Mark and Pat were both somewhat stabilized through weekly individual sessions, antidepressant medications, and continued involvement in AA and Al-Anon. They both continued to have many dissatisfying interactions with family, friends, and co-workers. Their ability to trust their psychotherapist was growing, although this trust was difficult to maintain outside the therapeutic relationship. Moments of conflict or difference with others continually threatened their newfound understanding of themselves, and memories of prior abusive interactions led to resumed abuse of self or others. It was recommended that both join my weekly psychotherapy group. Both were assured that the kinds of difficulties they were encountering in their social world would reappear in an intensive group. The added advantage of my providing input that they might not have considered while being involved in the emotional heat of the moment was emphasized.

EMILY

Emily is a middle-aged, divorced mother of one young child, and the oldest of five sisters. Her parents are both recovering alcoholics, and she married and divorced a man who was a substance abuser and had a history of impulsive behavior. Her father was hospitalized because of a suicide attempt in her early adolescence, and her husband suffered the same fate while they were married, which led her to seek individual psychotherapy. Her parents divorced in her early adulthood and she remains plagued by a sense of responsibility for their distress.

Emily is a professional woman with significant work responsibility who relates in a very cultured, articulate fashion. Her fear of closeness was apparent from the outset, although, like Mark and Pat, she was open regarding her concerns. In the initial stages of treatment she was also recommended to the Al-Anon program, and began benefiting almost immediately from the sense of not being alone in her reactions. Emily's strong tendency to internalize aggression and conflict became apparent in early sessions, as well as her wanting to please and be liked. Her core fear seemed somewhat different from those of Mark and Pat. Rather than being primarily focused on being humiliated or abandoned, she seemed more fearful of being physically hurt. She had humiliation and abandonment fears, but her strong sensitivity to being harmed was almost at a physical level. Her history did not indicate physical abuse, but rather highlighted barriers between her parents and herself. She vacillated in early treatment between her fear of her mother's relentless anger and her preoccupation with her father's unusual emotional distance from her. She remained in close contact with both parents and her siblings. These interactions, however, consistently seemed fraught with mixed messages and resultant self-doubt on her part. Her mother's unending rage toward men was unnerving, and her father's practical, methodical solution to emotional problems left her longing for warmth, understanding, and acceptance amid clear boundaries that would prove safe and secure.

Emily's depression was responsive to individual sessions, although it took some time before she could say that she was not depressed and had more available energy. She felt safe talking about relations outside of therapy, but was uneasy whenever any concerns arose in the room. She studied my reactions and worked hard to ascertain whether I was trustworthy, although this was very difficult for her to address directly. Eventually, she told me of her great sensitivity to her body image, and began telling more of how she restricted her food intake in what she realized was an unhealthy manner. Emily does not drink or smoke, and she does not exercise or participate in any mind–body activity to enliven her health.

Emily's trust in individual therapy was a good progressive sign. There was also concern, however, that she may hide from most other relationships outside her family unless she could develop greater confidence in her ability to relate to and assess men accurately. It was decided that she would join group therapy in an effort to risk and grow within the safety of a therapeutic milieu, under the leadership of her individual psychotherapist.

· ROD

Rod is a middle-aged father of two, suffering from alcoholism and abusive behavior to his wife. Rod had participated in a program for male offenders based on behavioral principles, with limited success. He continued to binge drink. He had discontinued physical violence, but frequently had screaming arguments with his wife. Rod is a professional like his alcoholic father, whom he emulates for his business success and quick mind. His mother is also alcoholic and was frequently the object of his father's verbal sadism. Rod also was humiliated and verbally demeaned by his father, whom he both resented and admired. He admired the power his father could hold over himself and others. He grew to idealize his father's intellect, never understanding how his father's sadism masked his insecurities. His core sensitivity, although having similarities with those of Pat, Mark, and Emily, was more indicative of his fear of being outsmarted. His frequent rationalizations for being late, missing sessions, or not paying the bill were all clear attempts to outsmart and gain leverage in the therapeutic relationship. He later disclosed, when these behaviors were consistently interpreted, that he would relate to his father in very similar ways, although he always felt guilty about his approach.

Rod accepted these interpretations when they were phrased in a manner that allowed him to see the sequential patterns in his behavior. Interpersonal balance again became crucial, as he was expecting punitive reactions when he acted out his feelings. Firm limits were established, but not without explanations indicating an understanding of his back door approach, which was explained as an adaptation made to avoid being demeaned by his father, thus addressing his fear of humiliation and feeling "less than." He valued empathic explanations that displayed lack of irritation with him, and he also respected the establishment of firm parameters in psychotherapy. In other words, he became interested in the process by which one can assert oneself and be firm, and yet not have any intent to hurt. He became interested in understanding the relational components of his disturbance and in learning the interactional ingredients that could lead him to the confidence to assert himself based on self-worth rather than through manipulations. Most important, he began to think that he was not inherently bad and deceptive, and that these behaviors were learned as a means of surviving and maintaining his sense of self.

It was also suggested to Rod that he join group sessions to further accentuate this process, and to experiment with the relational anxieties that led to binge drinking and aggressive acting out in the past. Each potential participant is told that the relational frustrations they bring to individual therapy are likely to be reexperienced in the group setting. Instead of reporting about conflicts and resultant sensitivities in their social world, we have the opportunity to explore the immediate origins of sensitivities engendered by group interactions, and to concurrently develop alternative coping strategies.

Rod, like Emily, was not referred for medication consultation as both showed progressive signs of their depression lifting. Rod's diet was poor, high in sugar intake, and he neither exercised nor participated in any other health-enhancing activity. He had belonged to health clubs in the past and at one time had practiced meditation, but had abandoned all these efforts over recent years.

BOB

Bob is middle-aged and currently separated from his wife of eight years. He has two younger brothers. Bob is a recovering alcoholic who was referred after a brief admission for detoxification. He was referred for group therapy, but was judged to be too unstable to manage an intensive group; thus, individual therapy was initiated to establish a much-needed therapeutic alliance. Bob's difficulty with maintaining appropriate boundaries was readily apparent in our first meeting. His tendency to invade the space of another was a means he used to try to establish immediate closeness and temporarily remove the threat of interpersonal anxiety. He immediately called me by my first name and at the end of the consultation put his arm around my shoulders as we walked down the hallway. Bob initially denied any conflict in his family, but eventually described his mother as perfectionistic. She always worried about the reflection her sons would have upon her, especially her oldest son. He described his father as a "nice man" who was relatively unsuccessful in business, but nevertheless was experienced as caring and interested in his family. Bob grew up in a middle-class town, attended state college, and then entered the corporate world. He felt at a definite disadvantage compared to colleagues who came from more affluent backgrounds, believing that they had decided advantages in procuring clients. He married a woman of stature whom he described as cultured and constantly trying to teach him how to behave, which he described as demeaning and making him angry. Her father was an alcoholic, with whom she had an intensely ambivalent relationship.

Bob's initial reaction to individual therapy was to want answers and concrete examples of how to succeed in his career and in his marriage. He paid close attention to my responses to him and attempted to develop a friendly feeling between us as a means of reducing any difference in the room. He was easily offended and displayed his aggressive side whenever he perceived being put down. My interpretation of his aggression as a defense was initially greeted with disdain, and on one occasion he referred to me as "Mr. Rogers." He eventually came to acknowledge his fears of inadequacy as he began to feel less threatened by the possibility of my viewing him in a demeaning manner. He slowly began to recognize his vulnerabilities and how he instantly became aggressive and offensive in order to protect his fragile sense of self. He started to utilize AA more readily and began working with a sponsor in a more constructive manner. He would frequently make reference to their conversations about women, inviting me to side with them in their disdain for and fear of heterosexual relating. Once sobriety had been fairly solidly established, he was transitioned to group therapy and continued in individual therapy twice a month.

Bob was 25 pounds overweight at the time, ate poorly (often fast food), with high sugar consumption. He had a history of dieting unsuccessfully and he would usually return to excessive alcohol use and abandon any health efforts. Bob drank in relation to conflict, consistent with Rod in that they both binged when feeling offended by their wives or co-workers. He had given up exercise after college and was fairly isolated socially, except for his wife's friends.

Bob slipped on two occasions in early group therapy sessions as he acted out after feeling offended by females who questioned his aggressive, confrontational style.

GROUP PSYCHOTHERAPY

Group A

Mark and Pat both belonged to the same group and the dynamics that have emerged between them have been both painful and growth promoting. The group generally consists of eight members of similar ages and similar self-worth levels. The theoretical persuasion of the therapist was examined in detail in the previous chapter.

Mark began his group experience with impatience, affected by the "slow pace" of sessions. He was reluctant to reveal his irritation for fear of being perceived as too aggressive and self-centered. He had been accused of egocentricity and impulsiveness many times, and was committed to not reinforcing the perceptions that fueled his self-hatred. As treatment evolved, his recovery solidified and depression became more pronounced. His method of soothing himself in the face of conflict was gone, with no immediate substitute. His guilt increased as memories of his drinking behavior became clear, producing much regret and self-loathing. In group interactions, he tried desperately to be rational and was able to be fair with others, but not with himself. His father died (they had not been speaking), and he had yet to speak to his mother after a falling out prior to his sobriety.

Mark responded to my providing a balanced reflection of himself, neither sugar coating his abusive acts nor siding with the extremes of his self-hatred. Most important, he responded to a more expansive explanation of his behavior that left him with a greater desire for self-understanding, as opposed to simply calling himself names that cut short attempts to explore causality and develop remedies. He had begun the critical process of substituting his punitive conscience with the reality-oriented understanding of the therapist's voice. He came to understand that his angry reactions were not just the product of his "aggressive nature," but rather were a means of defending himself from fears of humiliation and potential loss of control. The origins of fears were eventually explored as empathy, clear boundaries, and firm therapy parameters allowed him to feel safe enough to expose his vulnerabilities without falling apart internally.

Pat, on the other hand, started her group experience with anxiety and enthusiasm. She began in the role of helper, particularly trying with extreme patience and understanding to reach out to men, especially men who were not emotionally available. She felt rejected quickly as these men were not particularly responsive. They tended to view her espousing of taking "small steps" toward growth as unmanly and too emotional. They wanted fast gains without belaboring emotions.

Pat, through empathic interpretations that followed the sequences of her enabling behavior, eventually became more reflective of her input. However, she continued to feel somewhat rejected. It was as if she were hearing these comments as taking away her way of being. The sequence that led to her search for the protection of men was usually indicative of her highly developed ability to sense conflict brewing in the room. She additionally knew how to address the "fragile self" of the aggressive, cerebral male. On occasion, I would ask her what she was experiencing before she spoke, before she intervened. Her usual reply was, "I don't know." We eventually came to understand that this meant "I'm scared," scared of the potential aggression in the room, and scared of having responded in a manner that would displease the leader. It was at these moments that Pat's self-abuse became evident, providing the greatest opportunity for reversing this trend. Her sense of hurt needed to be gently examined, as her identity and worth were perceived as being challenged. Her conviction that she must soothe a man's ego to gain his love was not seen as intrinsic to being female, but rather examined in terms of learned behavior.

Many discussions in these groups revolve around gender stereotypes, role fixation, and cultural pressures. We have witnessed many remnants of gender rigidity represented by the perceptions that women provide nurturing for the emotional aspects of interactions while men solve problems by taking action and by being clear strategists.

Men do not allow emotion to get in the way of their thinking; women do not allow their thought patterns to ignore their emotional life. These generalities then are explored in terms of their accuracy and their origins. Alternative possibilities develop as a result of the group leader's positive relationship with members that has been solidified by the kind of exploration in individual therapy.

Pat, for instance, had experienced hurts in individual sessions that were both understood historically and changed in the here and now. The historical root of her reaction was important to explain, but the manner of explanation was even more important. Her sensitivity to the end of sessions, or particularly to the therapist's vacations, was understood in terms of her father's suicide and ex-husband's leaving. It was ultimately more important, however, that she did not feel "blamed" for her "childish reaction," but understood in a manner that she had seldom experienced. The therapist's prolonged and concentrated efforts to understand provided the safety for her and Mark to enter group interactions with less defensiveness and more acknowledgment of their vulnerabilities.

Pat and Mark are examples of two individuals who would not have been able to maintain themselves in an intensive group experience without individual therapy as a foundation. Both suffered from major depressions, abuse, and the internal or interactional effects of alcoholism. Recently in a group session, they both were examining when their relationship changed and they became positively attached to each other. This was prompted by very progressive and courageous work Mark had accomplished at a recent family gathering, where alcohol flowed and the opportunities to discharge aggressively were plentiful. He had reacted with poise, clarity of thought, assertion, and warmth. It was an improvement and Pat was complimenting him.

Pat had commented that although she was initially afraid of him and was trying valiantly to refrain from being his therapist, his growing ability to acknowledge his vulnerability brought her closer. She witnessed the aggression melt, and what remained was a man who suffered, as she did, but from a slightly different perspective. She spoke of wishing her father and ex-husband had had the courage to let their guard down and expose their hurt for healing. Conversely, Mark explained that her clear boundaries allowed him to feel cared for without stimulating his fear of being constantly criticized by an overbearing mother. He talked of his resonance to her description of her father's suicide and how this frightened him, for he had similar thoughts. Ironically, these moments of group despair, when faced squarely and with guidance, provided a map out of the maze of depression. The ability to manage interpersonal conflict became the key to depression-free living without despair.

Mark and Pat have studied the group leader's manner of managing intensity and conflict in the room. They have been particularly observant at times when aggression or disappointment is directed toward the leader. The expectation that conflict results in either abuse of self or another has been dominant. Many interactions of interpersonal balance have been necessary to enliven the potential for assertive conflict resolution in the face of intensity. Mark and Pat have gradually accessed this sense of balance, and both manage to assess themselves realistically at times of emotional intensity. The old patterns of returning to characteristic aggression or withdrawal are still present, but are less entrenched and less rigid.

As Mark and Pat evolve toward greater internal and interpersonal balance, their interest in overall health increases. Mark, with high blood pressure and high cholesterol, has been helped to develop a sound nutrition and exercise plan that he has maintained and is beginning to experience as a part of his life. Pat has come to understand her need for relaxation and self-nurturance, and has developed regimens that allow her to feel more connected socially and spiritually. Both have learned what is missing and important in their lives. Although Pat and Mark have lessened the likelihood of clinical depression, both continue to work on relational balance and overall fitness. These are two individuals who have displayed inordinate courage to face their vulnerabilities openly and thus grow in their efforts to obtain a higher quality of life.

Group B

Emily, Bob, and Rod have been integral and representative members of a second group. Emily's strong tendency to self-abuse had been observably matched by both men's tendency to project blame and disown responsibility for their lives. These entrenched behavioral patterns initiated all three into the group. It became readily apparent to group members that these modes of perception were predictable, while stimulating energetic responses in all members. In the beginning, sides would be subtly drawn along gender lines, progressively changing to perception based on actual rather than projected behavior.

Emily and Bob frequently engaged in heated interchanges, while Rod remained on the sidelines. Rod continued his indirect approach to relationships, identifying with Bob, but considering himself wise to react more diplomatically or not at all. As stated earlier he managed tension with others primarily through drinking, isolating, and acting out in a passive-aggressive manner. He occasionally forgot appointments, missed payments, or arrived late. He had been severely criticized by his wife for such behaviors and he both expected to be chastised and invited it. Interpretations in individual therapy focused on these behaviors as a means of coping with his ambivalence about both parents. This provided a palatable explanation rather than simply labeling him a manipulator, which he had heard many times. He grew to appreciate that labeling and diagnosing overt behavior is relatively uncomplicated; the real work comes with attempts to understand behavior with its functional origin. All three individuals and all group members had learned to label themselves negatively; none, however, had been guided to understand that their behavior was not intrinsic, but learned.

Chapter 1 detailed theoretical differences of this model in terms of explaining gender-based assertions of abuse of self and others. We do know that men are more likely to act out aggression and women are more prone to internalize it. The theoretical difference with classical analytic theory is that these behaviors have no innate base. Rod's indirect approach to others was both a learned manner of calming anxiety and maintaining distance with people to keep himself free from vulnerability. He has responded well to individual therapy as he clearly benefits when sequences of his acting-out behaviors are understood in terms of their historical and current relevances. His behavior has been so automatic since childhood that it has taken time for his awareness to increase to the point of engendering change. He remains quite reserved in group sessions, preferring to be cautious in his reactions, although his efforts increase gradually. His tendency to flee is quite strong, making group therapy a difficult and risky enterprise. Women in the group have perceived him as passive, which has continued to puzzle and impress him. His ideal view of himself is made up of identifications with his forceful father and the idea that his presence has been viewed as less than powerful hurts. Rod has explored this dynamic individually, and recently has worked harder to address this tendency in group. He has come to realize that his lack of directness is frequently perceived as a lack of caring. His fear of closeness can be misconstrued as aloofness and lack of interest.

Emily's reactions to Rod have been less intense than those to Bob. She has frequently told Rod that she feels that she does not know him and she can understand how his wife feels neglected. He usually reacts by saying that these comments are unfounded and gives testimonies of his concern for his wife and group members. Over time, however, he has not been able to deny group consensus of both males and females that he remains on the periphery and seems removed. Ultimately, there has been more acceptance of his fears of being less capable than others. He has acknowledged his anxieties and has felt more accepted and involved. He has relapsed during treatment, but has maintained sobriety for longer periods than ever before, and recently began a nutritional and exercise program. There is much work to do, but he has demonstrated that he is willing to take advantage of the opportunity at hand.

Emily's fixed perception of Bob as a typical aggressive, insensitive male, coupled with his perception of her as a liberal feminist who "hates men," has made for many intense interactions familiar to both parties. She represented the "cultured" wife and perfectionistic mother whom he could not please, and he represented her bright father and ex-husband, who both abused alcohol and blamed others for their fate.

Eventually, as both became stabilized in individual therapy through empathic focus on the origins of their biases, clarity of perception began to develop. He was intrigued by a therapist whom he experienced as neither aggressive nor demeaning, yet firm and assertive in setting much-needed limits and boundaries with him. She became more at ease as her suspicions of men were lessened through the consistency and persistency of therapeutic efforts.

Group interactions were obviously more taxing for both, as trust was not established, and both were keenly aware of how much they could be hurt by each other. In addition, and to their surprise, an attraction developed between them. They confirmed the old adage, "Some people get their loving from fighting." It became imperative to understand the evolution of this attraction, as both stated on many occasions that they wanted relationships without the same conflict as with their spouses. Emily and Bob were helped gradually to recognize their wish to return to the "scene of the crime." They both unconsciously longed to correct the hurts of their childhoods through choosing a spouse who could represent parental characteristics. This dynamic fueled the wish to symbolically change their familial history. The impossibility of this wish being granted was interpreted for both Emily and Bob in individual and, eventually, group sessions. This recognition in intensive psychotherapy is usually mandatory for progressive change to take place. Essentially, the longings for hurts of the past to be mended through parental representatives chosen in the present is a dysfunctional belief that brings much emotional pain. This phase in treatment is accompanied by mourning for lost wishes and regretful choices that were based on impossible premises.

Emily and Bob have grown to understand the nature of their attraction, although both remain fearful of future choices. They stimulate much less emotion in each other currently, and are more accepting of each other. They understand each other's vulnerabilities and respond less personally as a result. Bob has freed up energy in the process to manage his weight constructively, and Emily has become less preoccupied with restricting food intake as a means of expressing herself.

These five individuals have been highlighted to demonstrate a sense of the possibilities this psychotherapy model can provide. These individuals would not have benefited from either group or individual therapy in the same comprehensive manner if only one modality was employed. They would also have been compromised if two different psychotherapists were utilized. This model provides a unique opportunity to combine intrapsychic and interpersonal therapeutic work for those who have suffered abuse of self or others, and have consequently developed addictions or have chosen addicted partners.

Individual therapy is the key to beginning the process that shores up a fragile sense of self. Group psychotherapy continues the progression to the development of a resilient self that can manage interpersonal conflict successfully. Interpersonal relations can damage one's selfhood, and interpersonal therapeutic relations can repair and develop the self. Holistic health is approachable when stability of the self exists and is not constantly threatened. A holistic perspective of this process involves the establishment of an internal meta-voice that becomes neutral, aware, and self-editing—holistic in that it is not symptom based, but client resource based. Individual and group psychotherapy promote movement that expands this voice. The holistic process goal is not just removal of pain, but increased range of felt choices.

༼ 5 ༽

Holistic Health:
What Works?

The reader has been guided through therapeutic pathways that lead to the evolution of a solid sense of self as individuals release their attachment to unhealthy addictions and behaviors, and become active rather than passive learners about various aspects of their lives. It is impressive to witness the gradual interest patients develop in overall health, as their internal sense of anxiety is transformed into a feeling of inner tolerance and pride. The improvement in self-esteem and a coherent sense of self create a search for and learning of ways to maintain that new, energetic sense of self. Nutrition, exercise, and interpersonal relations hold us together as a self—body, mind, and spirit. To support self-care and wellness, there is an educative function we need to include in a complete model of care. We must emphasize the use of skills that can integrate the potential of the holistic health movement. Fostering these habits increases sustained change, internal locus of control, and ongoing care and health.

As the recovering person becomes interested in health he looks to the professional who has guided the recovery process for cues and monitoring. The individual is still prone to perfectionistic thinking and the idealization of others who seem to live a balanced life. Clinicians must facilitate continued progress beyond recovery from substance abuse to a way of thinking that allows the individual to comprehend and assess the array of information about health that is available to most people on a daily basis.

Malcolm Knowles, one of the leading experts in adult education, calls for a new emphasis on the development of proactive learners as compared to the traditional example of reactive learners who acquire knowledge passively without developing the ability to inquire and adapt to an ever-changing informational landscape (Knowles and Klevins 1987). He emphasizes that change in the information age will be the only consistent aspect of learning, as skill levels and information rapidly become obsolete. In many ways the qualities that Knowles and other innovative educators describe are often the desired outcome of an intensive psychotherapy effort. The progressive psychotherapist and educator both attempt to engender a process by which individuals develop skills that allow for adaptation to change based on the foundation of what psychoanalyst Heinz Kohut called a cohesive sense of self. The cohesive sense of self allows for internal consistency, in terms of one's identity, while also allowing for reasonable management of anxiety in the face of change. In other words, one has the faith that through initiative, motivation, and competent self-direction new challenges can be mastered and new learning can be integrated into an ever-expanding self.

In the information age change is a constant and people must learn how to adapt to an ever-evolving knowledge base. People who can cope with change will prosper; those who can't will be overwhelmed. Abused and addicted individuals are unable to take advantage of educational opportunities or health advancements. Their enfeebled sense of self does not allow for the integration of new information without undue anxiety and internal fragmentation. An interpersonal group psychotherapy model can help patients establish an internal structure that will enable them to integrate new opportunities without producing intolerable anxiety states. Health news demands thoughtful assessment. This chapter discusses recent information about holistic health and fitness. Fitness is an overall state of good health and well-being resulting from caring for the body, mind, and spirit as an integrated whole. Fitness is sometimes described as physiological ability, which is determined by such measures as the oxygen uptake test. These measures indicate an individual's ability, while running on a treadmill, to absorb and transport oxygen with healthy heart, lungs, and blood, as fit muscles combine oxygen with sugar and fat to procure efficient energy. Fitness, as a comprehensive entity, however, involves physical ability as well as emotional balance and maintaining purpose and meaning in life. The following sections update recent developments in exercise regimes; nutrition; vitamin, herb, and hormone supplements; alternative medicine; and the role of altruism and spirituality as pertains to health.

EXERCISE

The benefits of exercise in terms of quality of life and longevity are well established, but there is some confusion regarding its type, length, and frequency. Ralph Paffenbarger and his colleagues are responsible for the now famous Harvard Alumni Study, which has followed the health of approximately 22,000 men for as long as thirty-three years. This study has become well-known for being unusually comprehensive and for establishing guidelines of health for men. Its findings have indicated that life expectancy increased markedly as expenditure of calories increased from 500 to a maximum of 3,500 a week. Men aged 45 to 84 who took up moderate exercise had a 23 to 29 percent lower death rate than their sedentary classmates, with a 41 percent reduction in coronary heart disease. It has also been established that regular exercise raises the good high-density lipoprotein (HDL) blood cholesterol, lowers blood pressure, boosts immunities, and is preventive in terms of chronic illness like diabetes. A recent update of this study, published in the *Journal of the American Medical Association*, revealed that maximum longevity was attained by those exercisers who expended 1,500 calories a week in activities such as walking, jogging, cycling, and swimming. The death rates of alumni who expended 500 calories a week in vigorous exercise were 103 in 10,000 men, as compared to 1,000 calories expended per week with 96 deaths per 10,000. Individuals who expended 1,000 to 1,500 calories per week reduced their death rate to 75 per 10,000 (Knox 1995).

Recently JoAnn Manson, co-director of women's health at Brigham and Women's Hospital in Boston, gave an update of the 73,000 women studied in the Nurses' Health Study. Her presentation at the American Heart Association meetings showed that women who exercised for one hour, four or five times per week, had a 56 percent lower risk of stroke and a 44 percent lower risk of heart attack than those women who exercised for 20 minutes or less per week.

Journalist Judy Foreman (health science writer for the *Boston Globe*) recently wrote a very informative summary of the February 1996 meetings of the Centers for Disease Control and the American College of Sports Medicine meetings that attempted to review the literature on exercise and fitness, and establish health guidelines for adults.

I-Min Lee, epidemiologist from the Harvard School of Public Health, studied the same data from the Harvard Alumni group of Ralph Paffenbarger. She reaffirmed the 1,500 calorie a week guideline in that it reduced the risk of death by 25 percent compared to those who expended 150 calories per week. Vigorous activity is defined as individuals exercising in their personal target heart rate. This formula is deduced by subtracting your age from 220 to get your maximum heart rate. Target heart rate is determined by computing 65 to 80 percent of that figure. For instance, a 50-year-old woman would have a maximum heart rate of 170 and a target range of between 110 and 136.

Differences of opinion were expressed at the conference about I-Min Lee's assertion that nonvigorous activities reaped no benefit in decreasing mortality rates. Steven Blair, director of the Cooper Institute of Aerobics Research, challenged this assertion with his research on 10,000 men and 3,000 women who took treadmill tests rather than responding to questionnaires (Harvard Alumni Study). He found that the least fit group died at a rate of 64 per 10,000, moderately fit individuals died at a rate of 26 per 10,000 and this figure decreased to 20 per 10,000 in the most fit group. The figures for women were respectively 40, 16, and 7. The Cooper Institute maintains guidelines based on Blair's 1989 report that would call for 30 minutes of continuous activity, three to four times per week, to reduce mortality of all causes (Cooper 1994). We will explore Kenneth Cooper's innovative work on the role of antioxidants and vigorous exercise in a later section of this chapter.

Researchers may differ in their definitions of vigorous exercise. I-Min Lee's calculations are slightly lower than the formula used above, as her vigorous target rate for the same 50-year-old woman would be 100 to 135 heartbeats. Nevertheless, researchers agree that becoming physically active is necessary to maintaining quality of life and longevity. The Centers for Disease Control report that the ideal exercise program consists of 30 minutes of aerobic exercise per day in the target range in order for the average person to expend 1,500 calories per week. In addition, most experts would additionally advise strength training sessions to combat osteoporosis, to maintain muscle tone, and to abide by the old adage, "muscle burns more calories than fat." Kenneth Cooper, in his book, *Preventing Osteoporosis*, reports that bone loss occurs at a rate of 1 percent a year after the mid-thirties and escalates for women who have completed menopause (1989). Regular weight-bearing exercise is essential for preventing bone loss and allowing individuals to continue to perform physical tasks. It is quite remarkable how weight training can preserve muscle tone and strength throughout the life cycle with far less effort than once believed. A recent University of California at Berkeley Wellness Letter (1996a) highlighted studies demonstrating that one set of exercises as compared to the traditional three or more sets was all that was necessary for the average person to build and maintain strength.

In January 1996 the International Society of Exercise and Immunology made an attempt to put exercise in perspective by showing that the benefits of regular exercise are obvious, but excessive workouts increase levels of cortisol, a hormone that is an immunosuppressant that increases during mental and physical stress. The release of this hormone is thought to account for the increase in colds and flu symptoms after marathons and exercise that exceeds 90 minutes (Foreman 1996a). In addition, research at the Cooper Aerobics Center found that excessive exercise releases free radicals, which also impair immune function. Researchers at this center recommend running no more than fifteen miles per week, for instance. Antioxidant treatment will be discussed in a following section.

To maximize time spent exercising, *interval training* and *cross training* should be utilized as methods of enhancing fitness without increasing time spent in workouts. Interval training is defined as alternating bursts of exercise intensity (height of target range, 80 percent) to lower levels of exertion (low-end of target range, 60 percent) while recovering. Researchers at the Human Performance Laboratory at the University of Miami conducted studies that indicated that interval training produced greater gains than continuous aerobic exercise at a consistent pace; 18 percent gains were reported for interval trainers compared to 8 percent gains experienced by those participating in continuous exercise at the same steady level of exertion.

Cross training is defined as alternating exercise routines so that you are essentially doing more than one

physical activity on a regular basis, such as combining running three times per week with strength training twice a week. Running, which develops the hamstring muscles, is often alternated with bicycling, which develops the quadriceps, thus creating muscle balance and achieving the benefit of using more muscle groups than would be the case with only one exercise. Cross trainers tend to be better conditioned individuals than those who restrict themselves to one activity, although performance in any given sport will be better if individuals perfect particular sets of motion. Exercise for peak performance in one activity should not be confused with comprehensive fitness programs. Cross training works best when activities are chosen to complement each other; swimming strengthens the upper body while cycling strengthens the lower body (University of California at Berkeley Wellness Encyclopedia 1995).

Patients recovering from addictions should be aware that attaining a healthy level of fitness is accomplished through entering a learning process akin to recovery. Developing patience and tolerance of gradual gains must replace the addict's characteristic impulsive, perfectionistic behavior. Surveys have found that 25 percent of individuals beginning an exercise program quit within a week and 25 percent quit before six months; 1.4 million people join health clubs and never show up even once (Huebner 1996). Becoming fit is a complicated process and a lifelong learning experience. The active learner expects to learn and integrate new knowledge gradually and continually without the unnecessary complications of a punitive conscience demanding results by adhering to idealized criteria that cannot possibly be reached.

There is an abundance of evidence that regular exercise maintains a healthy heart, maintains aerobic and strength capacity, increases bone density, improves the immune system and neurological functioning, and protects against weight gain. In fact, in a recent study by Paul Williams, Ph.D., director of the National Runners' Health Study, thirty-five pairs of identical twins were compared for active and sedentary exercise activity. The sedentary twins ran less than 5 miles per week compared to the active twins who averaged running 39 miles per week. The study indicated that thirteen pairs of the sedentary twins were overweight compared to the more active twins. Additionally, good cholesterol (HDL) levels were significantly different for the runners, leading the research team to conclude that exercise apparently overcompensated for the genetic tendency to be overweight (Williams 1996).

George Sheehan, noted writer, runner, and cardiologist, once stated that he was one drink away from being an alcoholic before he returned to running and fitness in his forties. He, ironically, trained less and took more days for recovery as he aged, and at age 50 established the world record in the mile (4:45) for his age group and at age 61 ran his personal best marathon at 3:01, which is an incredible accomplishment at any age. Sheehan's results and Williams's twin studies are cited as examples of how age and genetics can be overcome, as well as noting that overtraining is counterproductive—it is often practiced by those with addictive, compulsive tendencies.

Overtraining can be avoided by alternating the intensity, duration, and type of exercise. Weight training, for instance, becomes counterproductive when the same muscle groups are worked daily; muscle simply needs time to repair. Runners run long distances at a relatively slow pace and run shorter distances at a faster pace; thus, one should take longer runs one week and shorter, less strenuous runs the following week. There is an established relationship with overtraining and sickness—excessive exercise produces the same distress that too little exercise can produce. We must then become students of our physiological cues, respecting the body's need for rest and the gradual, reasonable process that produces fitness (Bailey 1994).

NUTRITION

The University of California at Berkeley Wellness Letter updated its Wellness Encyclopedia (1995), providing several helpful guidelines regarding a healthy diet, as the editors caution from the outset that 40 percent of cancer occurrences in men and 60 percent in women are related directly to diet.

These guidelines highlight the need for fat intake to be at or below 30 percent of daily total calories, saturated fat to be less than one-third of the calories derived from fat, cholesterol intake to be 300 milligrams per day or less, 55 percent of daily diet to be derived from carbohydrates, and protein intake to be moderate (12 percent). One should consume a variety of foods, limit sugar and sodium, ingest adequate calcium, maintain reasonable weight, and consume no more than one ounce of alcohol per day. Antioxidant vitamin supplements are also recommended and will be discussed in the next section.

Researchers at the annual meeting of the North American Association for the Study of Obesity established the obvious fact that obesity is a complex process involving genetic and environmental interplay. It was stated in a review of this conference that 60 million Americans are classified as obese and 300,000 Americans die annually due to obesity, making this condition the second leading cause of preventable deaths next to tobacco. Although genes are seen as critical factors, the incidence of obesity has, nevertheless, increased from 25 percent in 1980 to 33 percent today, due to lack of exercise and the consuming of more calories (Foreman 1995b). This polemical dynamic is highly sensitive as thin individuals, who are not necessarily healthy, are envied for their ability to "eat anything and not get fat," whereas most of us have to work with some diligence to maintain weight. The cultural stereotype regarding ideal weight is enormously difficult to avoid, but there are also benefits to sound nutrition that supersede physical appearance.

High levels of energy, mental acuity, and sustained physical ability are the benefits that motivate good nutrition and fitness on a daily basis; if improved appearance follows as a by-product, it makes the effort seem even more worthwhile.

The University of California at Berkeley Wellness Encyclopedia (1995) and the Tufts University Guide to Total Nutrition (Gershoff 1990), as well as each university's monthly newsletter, present up-to-date nutritional information. There has been some recent confusion regarding protein, amino acids, and sugar intake. Protein supplements and high-protein diets continue to be recommended as a means of enhancing strength and adding muscle mass, thus aiding in weight management as muscle is known to burn calories, at rest and in activity. The above nutritional guides both indicate that there is no evidence to substantiate these claims, and, in fact, excess protein is utilized by the body for energy or it is converted to fat. Most protein supplements are high in calories, increasing the likelihood of weight gain and, additionally, can also produce negative effects, "chiefly dehydration, diarrhea, and calcium loss, and may aggravate liver or kidney disease as well" (University of California at Berkeley Wellness Encyclopedia 1995, p. 121). The current guidelines for protein intake can be calculated by 0.8 grams of protein per kilogram of body weight. A kilogram is equal to 2.2 pounds, thus a 170 pound man would divide his weight by 2.2 (77 kilograms) and multiply by 0.8 grams, which gives a result of 62 grams of protein as the daily requirement (Tufts Total Nutrition Guide 1990).

AMINO ACIDS

These are the building blocks of all proteins. The body requires all 22 amino acids; 12 of them can be produced by the body and are called nonessential, and the remaining 10, called essential amino acids, must be obtained from food. Recently, health publications and media spots have accented the idea that amino acids can offer natural mood regulators similar to the effects of antidepressants like Prozac and enhance serotonin production. Amino acids are precursors of natural neurotransmitters; for instance, the amino acid tryptophan is the precursor of serotonin and melatonin. Michael Murray, a naturopathic physician and author of *Natural Alternatives to Prozac* (1996), believes that amino-acid therapy is as effective as antidepressant medications. He highlights data indicating the beneficial effects of tryptophan, tyrosine, phenylalanine, S-adenosyl-methionine, and gamma-aminobutyric acid (GABA).

Tryptophan

Tryptophan was banned in the United States in 1989 when a Japanese manufacturer sold this amino acid not knowing that it had been contaminated. It later caused eosinophilia-myalgia syndrome (EMS) with muscle and joint pain, fever, swelling, and shortness of breath (Murray 1996). Murray believes that the Food and Drug Administration (FDA) overreacted in its decision to ban this amino acid, as it clearly raises levels of mood-enhancing neurotransmitters, such as serotonin and melatonin, which are thought to be natural antianxiety agents. Foods high in tryptophan are carbohydrates such as bananas, wheat, sunflower and pumpkin seeds, and baked potatoes with their skins.

Phenylalanine and Tyrosine

These are converted to phenylethylamine (PEA), a substance that Murray reports has amphetamine-like qualities and is thought to counter depression, based on the fact that some studies have found low PEA levels in depressed patients. Tyrosine is increased by high protein food groups such as lean red meat, poultry, tuna, egg whites, skim milk, legumes, and soy products. Tyrosine is an important component of the neurotransmitters norepinephrine and dopamine; both are factors in mental alertness and mental ability.

S-Adenosyl-Methionine (SAM)

This amino acid is reportedly present in limited amounts in depressed individuals. It increases levels of serotonin and dopamine and has been found to function quicker and more effectively than some antidepressants (Murray 1996). Double-blind studies comparing SAM to tricyclic antidepressants displayed the benefits of this amino acid over the traditional treatment, although it is not recommended for individuals with manic tendencies and is not yet available in the United States.

Gamma-Aminobutyric Acid (GABA)

This is described as a calming agent that is stimulated by benzodiazepines such as Valium; thus, the supplement is seen as an alternative for individuals who are addicted to benzodiazepines and as an agent that can induce sleep. GABA is manufactured in the body from the amino acid glutamate, vitamin B_6, and vitamin C. GABA plays an important role in relaxation and sleep and is thought by some to be a safer means of treating insomnia than using barbiturates or benzodiazepines.

Although amino acid supplements are recommended by some researchers and addiction specialists (Chaitow 1985, Erdmann 1989, Murray 1995) as alternatives to antidepressants and anxiety agents, others are quite cautious about their use. For instance, the amino acid glutamine has been recommended to curb the alcoholic's craving for sugar, which can precipitate return to an alcoholic cycle, and various amino combinations have been recommended in the treatment of anorexia (Erdmann 1989). Recent research has shown that exercise raises levels of tryptophan, the precursor of serotonin. Significantly high levels of serotonin can lead to fatigue and loss of focus, but when branched chain amino acids (BCAAs) (leucine, isoleucine, valine) are consumed they compete with tryptophan for access to the brain and ultimately reduce the levels of tryptophan reaching the brain. Studies have, in fact, shown that athletes who consume BCAAs supplements during performances became less tired than a control group (Arnot 1996).

Bob Arnot, M.D., in a recent article entitled, "Mind-Altering Protein" (1996), reports that best-selling books like *Protein Power* and *The Zone* are indications of the renewed interest in protein and amino acid influence on neurotransmitters. He cautions, however, that the FDA would probably ban such supplements if it were not for the heavy lobbying efforts. The FDA has not been convinced that amino supplements are safe and there are indications that BCAA supplements produce ammonia, which has a toxic effect on the brain and muscles. The safe alternative is to obtain amino acids from food groups, accenting tyrosine (egg whites, whey protein, tuna, red meat, poultry, legumes) for alertness and mental performance and tryptophan (bananas, sunflower seeds, pumpkin seeds, potatoes, and shredded wheat) for relaxation. Arnot reports that tryptophan, unlike tyrosine, cannot enter the brain without carbohydrate assistance.

Sugar's function and use requires clear understanding for ongoing health, particularly as it pertains to alcoholism and hypoglycemia. The University of California at Berkeley Wellness Encyclopedia clears up common misconceptions: (1) Sugar is not the primary cause of obesity; fat intake is more prominent. Fat in cakes and cookies is accountable for significantly more calories than sugar, and fat is far more accountable for the deleterious aspect of the American diet than sugar. (2) High sugar intake is not a risk factor in heart disease. (3) Excess sugar is not the cause of diabetes. Obesity is the leading risk factor for non–insulin-dependent diabetes. (4) True hypoglycemia is rare; few people with chronic fatigue and restlessness have low blood sugar levels. (5) Sugar eaten right before exercise is counterproductive, except when exercising more than two consecutive hours.

James Milam, in his now classic, *Under the Influence* (Milan and Ketcham 1981), encouraged addiction specialists to develop an appreciation for the alcoholic's chronic problem with blood sugar levels, citing that 95 percent of early- and late-stage alcoholics given a 5-hour glucose tolerance test have spikes in blood sugar levels after ingesting sugar followed by rapid drop in the levels. He cautioned that there is a great need for education in this area as blood sugar levels greatly influence irritability, depression, and insomnia while creating a strong craving for sugar that often leads to misunderstood relapses.

The hypoglycemic ingests sugar, and glucose levels rise normally but then drop unusually because the pancreas overproduces insulin. When sugar levels drop, the adrenal glands are alerted and adrenaline is released, thus causing anxiety and panic. Temporary relief is found through ingesting more sugar (alcohol), which restores glucose levels to normal, but unfortunately results in further drops hours later, producing the depressive cycle all over again. Author and recovering alcoholic Mark Gavreau Judge (1993) explains this process: Normal blood sugar levels are between 80 and 120. In his first glucose tolerance test his levels vacillated from 81 to 20 milligrams in the fourth and fifth hour of testing. It has been noted that the brain adapts to the constant presence of alcohol by using it as a fuel instead of glucose, altering the individual's ability to utilize glucose, which results in spikes and drops in circulating glucose levels (Beasley 1989). As mentioned previously, the amino acid glutamine is thought to aid in breaking the blood sugar cycle by affecting the appetite center located in the hypothalamus gland. This center is thought to respond by creating a craving whenever there is a shortage of a particular nutrient. If there are low blood sugar levels, then this appetite center creates a craving for sugar, which alcohol can satisfy easily. Glutamine is thought to break the cycle by suppressing messages that stimulate sugar cravings (Erdmann 1987). Glutamine is the precursor of the calming amino acid GABA. Hypoglycemia is managed through the elimination of refined sugar and by adhering to a diet high in protein and complex carbohydrates, which provides a consistent amount of glucose without causing the peaks and valleys of quickly absorbed sugar-bearing substances such as alcohol and sweets.

The role of nutritional guidance in determining health will continue to grow as new information becomes available. Rachael Heller, coauthor of *Healthy for Life* (1996), believes that research will provide diets for smaller subgroups according to results of blood tests and symptoms that reveal slightly different nutritional needs for particular individuals. Other experts believe physicians will prescribe foods more so for ailments and general health, and beneficial ingredients, like carotenoids and vitamins, will be implanted in crops through alteration of genes (Krajick 1996).

SUPPLEMENTS—VITAMINS, HERBS, HORMONES

Vitamins

The necessity of vitamin intake for good physical and mental functioning is well established. The reader is again directed to the nutrition newsletters and texts mentioned previously as comprehensive references. One area that has been debated is the need for vitamin supplements in the diet. The University of California at Berkeley Wellness Letter has traditionally been on the conservative side, although recently its editors have acknowledged that the collective research in recent years has caused a change in their thinking and they have now recommended taking the three antioxidant vitamins (E, C, and beta carotene) and folacin, citing that these vitamins clearly play a critical role in disease prevention.

Folacin has drawn attention recently as the FDA has reported that several grain products will be fortified with folacin by 1998. The University of California at Berkeley Wellness Letter (1996c) featured folacin in its headline article, reporting its use in preventing birth defects, cervical cancer, and heart disease. Women need 180 micrograms and men need 200 micrograms daily, while the needs of pregnant women rise to 400 micrograms (a microgram is one thousandth of a milligram). Foods rich in folacin are wheat germ, leafy green vegetables, beans, and brewer's yeast. One ounce of most breakfast cereals supply about 100 micrograms of folacin.

An antioxidant, on the other hand, is a vitamin, mineral, or amino acid that is thought to slow the process of oxidation (a chemical reaction that removes an electron from the compound being oxidized), which creates the infamous free radical, a compound that lacks an electron or is an unpaired electron. Free radicals are now linked to heart and blood vessel disease, cancer, cataracts, and acceleration of the aging process. Vitamins C, E, beta carotene (a derivative of vitamin A), and the mineral selenium have been the object of much research, and antioxidants have been recommended by many health experts as necessary supplements. The abounding research and media attention regarding antioxidants and free radicals has created enormous interest and ambiguity simultaneously. The most recent research has created further anxiety by reporting that strenuous exercise, such as marathon training, releases free radicals in abundance, possibly accounting for the high incidence of flu or cold outbreaks prior to the scheduled race. Kenneth Cooper, former marathon runner and author of *Antioxidant Revolution* (1994), cites several examples of highly trained runners becoming seriously ill, as well as research done at the Cooper Institute of Aerobic Research that shows that excessive exercise may release free radicals into the body, damaging muscles, liver, blood, and overall health. Cooper emphasizes the necessity of regular aerobic and strength training, but cautions against overtraining because of the growing data that correlate such exercise with the release of free radicals.

The University of California at Berkeley Wellness Encyclopedia recommends obtaining the necessary vitamins and minerals through diet, but recognizes that only 9 percent of Americans eat the five servings of vegetables and fruits needed. With this reality in mind, the editors advise taking 250 to 500 mg of vitamin C, 10,000 to 25,000 IU of beta carotene, and 200 to 800 IU of vitamin E. In contrast, Kenneth Cooper recommends 400 IU of vitamin E, 1,000 mg of vitamin C for women and 1,500 mg for men, and 25,000 IU of beta carotene for those 22 to 50 years old. He increases the amounts for those over 50 to 600

IU of vitamin E, 2,000 mg of vitamin C for men over 50, and 50,000 IU of beta carotene for the elder group.

Recently, the National Cancer Institute reported two new studies that revealed that beta carotene supplements have no benefit and may in fact be harmful. This news created immediate media attention and the University of California at Berkeley Wellness Letter (1996b) issued an addendum to their initial guidelines advising those who smoke not to use beta carotene supplements. Those who do not smoke can continue without harm, but would be better served by consuming carrots and carotenoids like oranges, tomatoes, and grapefruit, and limiting beta carotene supplements to 6 to 15 mg daily, as evidence still exists that beta carotene may "reverse certain pre-canceorus conditions" (p. 2).

There seems to be little question that consuming foods rich in beta carotene lowers risk factors for heart disease, cancer, and other diseases, but, as the University at California at Berkeley Wellness Letter (1996b) reports, taking beta carotene in pill form may not have the same result as food consumption, and for unknown reasons one study (subjects were selected for having a high risk of lung cancer) found that beta carotene supplements increased lung cancer rates for smokers. Andrew Weil, author of *Spontaneous Healing* (1995), has also discontinued his recommendation of taking beta carotene supplements based on the National Cancer Institute study and now recommends taking mixed carotene supplements that provide lycopene, which is found in tomatoes and is protective against prostate cancer, as are lutein, zeaxanthin, and alpha and beta carotene. He recommends 25,000 IU for both men and women (Weil 1996a). In the premiere edition of his newsletter *Self Healing*, Weil also recommends supplements of 4,000 to 6,000 mg of vitamin C for men and 3,000 to 5,000 mg for women, 400 to 800 IU of vitamin E as natural d-alpha-tocopherols, not synthetic d-alpha tocopherols. He further advises consuming 200 to 400 mg of selenium, 60 to 100 mg of Coenzyme Q, and 15 to 30 mg of zinc for both sexes. Ralph Golan, M.D., author of the comprehensive text *Optimal Wellness* (1995), cautions that selenium can be toxic over 500 micrograms per day, causing immunosuppression, hair loss, irritability, and fatigue. Golan additionally adds that zinc is usually safe up to 50 milligrams, but additional doses can also produce immunosuppression and digestive disturbances, and reduce copper levels. Selenium is an antioxidant mineral that works along with vitamin E to counter the effects of free radical damage, thus slowing aging and tissue breakdown. Zinc enhances the immune system, protects against other mineral toxicity, and is usually depleted in alcoholics, anorexics, diabetics, and those taking cancer drugs and antibiotics (Golan 1995).

Coenzyme Q-10 and chromium picolinate are supplements millions of Americans consume, although both substances are controversial. Joseph Pizzorno, naturopathic physician and president of Bastyr University, cites numerous research in his text, *Total Wellness* (1996), that indicates the positive role of Coenzyme Q-10 in preventing and reversing cardiovascular disease. It is also reported to increase aerobic activity, and the University of California at Berkeley Wellness Letter (1996f) indicates it is a powerful antioxidant that appears to be safe, although evidence of its coronary effectiveness is somewhat unclear.

Chromium was recently discovered as having a crucial role in blood sugar control, essentially aiding in turning carbohydrates into glucose. Studies have shown beneficial effects of helping those with hypoglycemia and in preventing diabetes. Additional research has found that chromium supplements can lower body weight and increase lean body mass (Murray 1994). Recently, however, a laboratory study conducted at Dartmouth College indicated that chromium picolinate causes chromosome damage. This study caused a furor on both sides of the issue, resulting in the authors of one of the studies concluding that the long-term effects of this supplement are not well understood. Although claims of the benefit of this supplement are enormous, prudence is again highly recommended (University of California at Berkeley Wellness Letter 1996). Due to insufficient scientific study, the Federal Trade Commission recently forced leading manufacturers of chromium picolinate to desist in their claims that it promotes weight loss, lowers cholesterol, burns fat, and builds muscle tone (University of California at Berkeley Wellness Letter 1997).

Other substances receiving wide acclaim are glucosamine and chondroitin sulfate, colloidal minerals, blue-green algae, essential fatty acids (EFAs) and phytochemicals.

Glucosamine is an amino sugar, a component of glucose. Chondroitin sulfate is also an amino sugar that promotes water retention in cartilage. These substances have come to the forefront as a result of the popular book *The Arthritis Cure* (1997) by Jason Theodosakis and colleagues. The authors' bold claims about the effectiveness of these substances in the treatment of osteoarthritis have been received with controversy.

The University of California at Berkeley Wellness Letter (1997) indicates that the text is filled with inaccuracies and errors in biochemistry. They do not recommend the substances, citing inconclusive research, but nevertheless indicate there may be no harm in trying these components for pain reduction.

Andrew Weil (1997), on the other hand, indicates anecdotal success treating patients with both substances as well as citing a study of 1200 participants where 95 percent of glucosamine and chondroitin users indicated a reduction in pain and an increase in ability.

Both critics encourage osteoarthritic sufferers to continue comprehensive programs of exercise, sound diet, and weight management.

The Arthritis Foundation does not recommend chondroitin sulfate and glucosamine, but rather supports the traditional programs cited above in addition to taking acetaminophen for pain relief (Shute 1997). The Foundation, along with Weil and the University of California Wellness editions, call for more extensive studies with larger numbers. Documented side effects of chondroitin sulfate and glucosamine have been limited to gastrointestinal upset thus far.

Colloidal minerals have been popularized recently by Joel Wallach's audiotaped lecture, *Dead Doctors Don't Lie* (1996). Wallach is a veterinarian and naturopath. His tape states that he was nominated for a Nobel Prize in Medicine in 1991. This tape has been sent to thousands of households throughout the United States with the hope of gaining mail order purchases for these minerals. Wallach claims that colloidal minerals are liquids that are 98 percent absorbable by the body. They have been converted by plants from metallic minerals, are reportedly 7000 times smaller than a red blood cell, and are 10 times more available for absorption than metallic minerals (ground up rocks, clays, and shells).

Weil (1997) indicates that leading experts in nutritional biochemistry seriously question claims of colloidal mineral absorption, stating that they certainly do not warrant their excessive cost compared to drug store brands of vitamin and mineral supplements. He also cautions against the ingestion of potentially toxic minerals that are listed in colloidal mineral products. He also questions claims that such minerals are deficient in most diets and can treat baldness, aneurysms, cardiomyopathy, and lower back pain.

Weil (1996b) and the University of Berkeley Wellness Letter (1997) also caution against the use of another widely publicized health wonder, blue-green algae. These tiny organisms are microscopic plants of bacteria and algae that include spirulina, anabena, and another variation called aphanizomenon. Supplements of blue-green algae contain mainly protein (60–70 percent), beta carotene, vitamin C, folacin, and chlorophyll.

Claims made by manufacturers that blue-green algae supplements cure AIDS, herpes, and Alzheimer's are unfounded. They consist mainly of protein, and we have no protein shortage in the United States. It also has the potential to release toxins into the system and complaints to consumer groups regarding side effects have been frequent. The marketing of blue-green algae is simply suspicious, and this substance does not warrant consumption.

Essential fatty acids (EFAs), on the other hand, are polyunsaturated fats that are essential parts of cell membranes, nerve cells, and hormone-like substances called prostaglandins. All fatty acids vary in the amount of saturation by hydrogenatons. This saturation level determines whether a fatty acid is monosaturated (olive, canola oils), polyunsaturated (corn, safflower oils), or highly saturated (coconut and palm oils).

Prostaglandins control inflammatory and anti-inflammatory processes in the body, as well as enhancing the immune and circulatory systems. They are affected by the kinds of fats and oils we ingest. Animal fat, for instance, contributes to the release of higher levels of inflammatory prostaglandin chemicals in the body. Diets high in fish, fish oils, or supplements of flax or borage oils result in the production of anti-inflammatory prostaglandins (Pizorno 1996).

Supplements such as evening primrose oil, flax seed oil, and black currant oil contain two essential polyunsaturated fats: linoleic and alpha-linolenic acid. These acids produce prostaglandins that are protective to health, while other fats and oils produce prostaglandins that are destructive. Hydrogenated oils (trans-fatty acids) release unhealthy prostaglandins. In excess these substances can lead to suppression of the immune system, high blood pressure, heart attacks, and stroke. Since there is considerable evidence that the American diet is now deficient in essential fatty acids it appears reasonable to supplement (Golan 1995).

Phytochemicals are substances in fruits and vegetables that are considered to be medicinal. Media reports abound as to the ability of these chemicals to prevent cancer. Isothiocyanates (found in cabbage and turnips), genistein (found in soy), and polyphenols (found in green tea and wine) have all been linked to cancer prevention.

The health food industry has capitalized on research indicating the positive role of phytochemicals by isolating certain chemicals and selling them in pill form.

Lycopene, for instance, a carotenoid in tomatoes, has been found to reduce the risk of prostate cancer. Additional research, however, indicates that unless tomatoes are eaten in oil, lycopene is not properly absorbed by the intestines. Isolating phytochemicals may not have the same benefit as simply eating fresh vegetables and fruit to combat cancer. The National Cancer Institute seriously questions manufacturers' zeal for bottling phytochemicals. They cite the controversy surrounding beta carotene as an example of how fruits and vegetables have hundreds of complex ingredients accounting for their effectiveness. Isolating one aspect in a pill may have positive or negative effects, as demonstrated by smokers who raised their risk of lung cancer by taking beta carotene supplements (University of California at Berkeley Wellness Letter 1996b).

Although phytochemical research holds much promise, it is premature to think that isolated compounds in pill form will effectively protect against various cancers (Hall 1997).

Herbs

Since herbs are not regulated by the FDA their popularity has led to much confusion about the claims manufacturers make regarding their efficacy. Some herbs have proven effective for a given function; others have proven dangerous. Unfortunately, many Americans still believe that if products are sold over the counter they are regulated, and this misconception has led the consumer to assume advertising claims must be scientifically based or the government would not allow the products to be sold. Additionally, herbs that have proved effective are not necessarily standardized, meaning that the consumer is not assured of potency, as may or may not be indicated on the label.

In 1995 estimated sales of herbal products were $2 billion and yet studies have indicated wide variance in terms of quality and consistency. Recently, *American Health* (May 1996) and *Consumer Reports* (November 1995) have published respective guidelines regarding herbs that are helpful and those that may be harmful. *American Health* based its report on the German federal health agency that established recommendations by a panel of experts reviewing clinical trials, and physician and patient reports, and *Consumer Reports* conducted its own evaluation of several products by various manufacturers. The FDA has also published a report on herbs they consider to be dangerous. Varro Tyler's book *Herbs of Choice* (1994) is also a credible reference guide.

Herbs with Positive Potential

Chamomile

This flower is thought to both aid in digestion and to reduce inflammation, as well as having a calming effect, which has led many people to drink chamomile tea before bedtime. People who are allergy sufferers are better off avoiding this herb, particularly those allergic to ragweed and members of the daisy family. Otherwise, it is considered to be quite safe and is usually taken as a tea that generally contains 10 to 15 percent of the oil contained in the flowers.

Garlic

Sales of garlic supplements worldwide have reached $250 million a year, as this popular herb has been acclaimed for its ability to lower cholesterol (9 percent in some studies), fight cardiovascular disease by reducing platelets in the blood from clotting, and boost immunities, and it has also been linked to fighting cancer as it has been demonstrated to slow cell growth (Foreman 1996c). Individuals taking anticoagulant drugs and those preparing for surgery are warned to discontinue use because of garlic's propensity for interfering with blood clotting. The University of California at Berkeley Wellness Letter (1996d) recently questioned the validity of garlic claims, although also indicated that it is not thought to be harmful. Researchers at Cornell University Medical College have set up the Garlic Information Center hotline at 1-800-330-5922.

Ginkgo

The number one prescription drug in Germany is derived from the ginkgo tree, which has reportedly been used for healing purposes by the Chinese for over 4,000 years. This herb is used to increase blood flow to the brain, to improve concentration, memory, and circulation, and to treat senility, impotence, and inner ear dysfunction. Ginkgo is generally regarded as safe if taken at a reasonable dose (24 percent flavonglycosides, 40 mg three times per day) as forty-four double-blind studies produced few side effects, the most common being gastrointestinal uneasiness (Murray 1996). In addition, ginkgo affects clotting and should be used cautiously by anyone taking anticlotting medications.

Saw Palmetto

Clinical trials in Germany and throughout Europe have attested to the effectiveness of this dark berry that is the product of a palm that grows in Southeastern United States (Wild 1994). This berry, when prepared as an oil base extract, is used to treat prostate enlargement (benign prostate hyperplasia). It aids in urinary flow, and has shown anti-inflammatory effects. Urologists caution, however, that men should not take this herb in lieu of a prostate examination and it should not be taken when prescription medications are also taken, as a negative interaction is possible.

Valerian

This plant is an upright perennial that grows in damp surroundings throughout Europe; extracts are taken from its root for treating anxiety and insomnia. Valerian has been approved in Germany for these functions, although the active ingredients are not known. Additionally, it has also been used to treat menstrual cramps and spasms, has a low incidence of side effects except when taken in unusually high doses, which can cause headaches and lethargy. Physicians with holistic backgrounds tend to use valerian as a first attempt to treat insomnia before using benzodiazapines like Valium. Dosages are generally 300 to 500 mg of concentrated valerian root standardized to 0.5 percent oil for insomnia, taken one hour before bedtime. Dosage for anxiety is usually 200 to 300 mg complemented by the evening dose cited above.

Echinacea

This wildflower was used before the advent of antibiotics as it boosts immunities by normalizing white blood cells, which helps fight bacteria and viruses. Echinacea should be taken at the first sign of flu or cold symptoms; a teaspoonful of alcohol-based tincture is sufficient. Use is not recommended for more than eight days as tolerance reduces effectiveness and it may also cause a reaction to those with allergies to the sunflower family.

Ginger

This old spice has been shown to be effective in treating motion sickness and it aids in digestion. One study of thirty-six college students found ginger to be more effective than Dramamine, with none of the drowsy side effects produced by the prescription drug (Wild 1994). Side effects of ginger have been rare, although there is some evidence that in large doses ginger can inhibit clotting. In the experiment cited, students took 940 mg of ginger, equal to two standard tablets.

Feverfew

Parthenolide, a compound found in feverfew, is effective in treating migraine sufferers. Feverfew cannot, however, be taken at the time of the onset of the migraine, but rather must be taken on a regular basis as a prophylactic. It is difficult to obtain products that contain parthenolide and it is necessary to ingest 0.2 percent of the active ingredient for positive results. It has been prescribed in 300 to 400 mg tablet doses without any known complications, although chewing the leaves of this plant can irritate and cause ulcers of the lips. It is also not recommended for those allergic to the daisy family. Those taking anticlotting medication should also not use feverfew as it may affect the clotting components of blood (Wild 1994).

Milk Thistle

This plant, found in the Mediterranean, has been used for 2,000 years in treating liver disorders. The substance silymarin, found in milk thistle seeds, protects the liver from damage, but is also known to regenerate liver tissue. This substance should not be used without supervision by a physician and capsules are the only effective manner of utilizing its positive properties.

Hawthorn

The fruit of this rose tree has been used for many years to dilate blood vessels, particularly the coronary arteries. The fruit is also used to lower blood pressure and may aid in the treatment of angina by relaxing muscles in coronary vessels. This herb should not be used without consulting a physician as it may interact negatively with prescription drugs for cardiac problems. It could, however, be added to conventional therapy if interactions are ruled out by a cardiologist.

St. John's Wort

This perennial plant has yellow flowers and is found in dry, rocky areas where sun is prevalent. Recently, this herb has caused much optimism as researchers at New York University found it to have dramatic action against the AIDS virus. The FDA has approved a study to determine the effects of its components on the virus and thus far results are encouraging, without side effects. St. John's Wort is also very promising in the treatment of depression; some think it is by far the most effective natural antidepressant available today (Murray 1996). Over 25 double-blind studies have been done comparing St. John's Wort to conventional antidepressants like imipramine and amitriptyline. This herb has surpassed effectiveness of the antidepressants while not interfering with sleep and producing no known side effects when used at the standard dose of 300 mg three times daily (Murray 1996). The plant is named after John the Baptist, with its red oil being symbolic of his blood. The herb is effective in aiding mild and moderate depression, but has not been used with major depression. Its active ingredient, hypercin, has also been effective in treating minor wounds (Wild 1994).

Ginseng

This root probably has been researched more than any other herb, with claims of its effectiveness ranging from increased endurance, to greater immunity, blood pressure regulation, and the treatment of impotence. On the other hand, it is difficult for the consumer to know what is being purchased as *Consumer Reports* (Herbal roulette 1995) reported that their investigation of ginseng products demonstrated wide variance among ten products for amounts of ginsenoside, the active component of ginseng. Recently, a study to test the effects of ginseng on trained runners was conducted with a control group. Results indicated that runners using ginseng had no advantages compared to those taking a placebo. Ginseng did not enhance oxygen use, lactate levels, heart rate, fat burning, or recovery time (Applegate 1996). The value of this age-old herb remains a mystery, although Russian scientists claim Siberian ginseng is useful for fatigue because it spares glycogen use in muscles by aiding the use of fatty acids as a fuel source. It has been reported that hypoglycemics should restrict large amounts of ginseng, and long-term use of ginseng should be followed by periods of abstinence for two weeks (Balch and Balch 1990).

Tea

Black tea contains caffeine (10 to 15 mg), and theophylline, both of which act as bronchodilators, helping in unclogging respiratory passages. Green tea, more often consumed in the Orient, supplies polyphenols, such as catechin, which is believed to be an antioxidant and cancer fighter, while polyphenols in general have been found to lower blood pressure and cholesterol in animal studies (Wild 1994).

Herbs with Negative Potential

Ephedra

Chinese physicians have used ephedra, also known as majuang or epitonin, for centuries to treat colds, asthma, and hay fever. It has also been used to treat obesity. It increases basal metabolic rate, stimulates the heart, but increases blood pressure, and can cause insomnia as a result. Pseudoephedrine, a derivative of ephedra, is the active ingredient in most decongestants, like Sudafed. Ohio has placed strict guidelines on the use of ephedra as an over-the-counter product as it led to the death of an adolescent in Ohio and the death of a Texas woman who purchased an ephedra-caffeine product. The FDA is currently investigating the dangers of ephedra as it has been known to cause nerve and muscle damage, stroke, and memory loss (*American Health*, May 1996, *Consumer Reports*, November 1996).

Chaparral

Native Americans used this desert shrub historically, and currently it is used as a tea or capsule that is claimed to be an antioxidant, cancer fighter, blood cleanser, and treatment for acne. The FDA has reported several cases of acute hepatitis, with permanent liver damage substantiated in two incidences.

Yohimbe

This bark of an African tree has recently been prescribed to offset the loss of sexual drive caused by selective serotonin reuptake inhibitors (SSRI)-type antidepressants like Prozac, and it has also been used to treat impotence, although clinical trials indicate it is ineffective. The state of Georgia has banned nonprescription use due to severe side effects if overdose occurs (*Consumer Reports*, November 1996).

Lobelia

This Indian tobacco functions like nicotine. In minimal doses it dilates the bronchial tubes and elevates respiratory rate. In high doses it can cause rapid heart rate, low blood pressure, restricted breathing, and coma.

Comfrey

Four countries—Australia, Canada, Great Britain, and Germany—limit access to this substance that was initially used for topical treatment of swelling caused by broken bones. Recently, it has additionally been used as a blood cleanser as well as a treatment for asthma, cough, cramps, and burns. It has now been linked to several cases of restricted blood flow from the liver, and there is one reported case of a pregnant woman who drank comfrey tea that resulted in liver disease in her baby.

Germander

This group of plants renders teas and capsules used for weight loss. France has reported many cases of acute hepatitis and the French government has eliminated its use (*American Health*, May 1996).

Willow Bark

Chinese physicians have used willow bark for centuries to relieve pain as it contains salicin, the active ingredient that was initially used by chemists studying willow bark to make aspirin in the nineteenth century. Varro Tyler, Ph.D., professor of pharmacognosy at Purdue University, cautions that the salicin content of willow bark varies considerably and that several cups of tea would be necessary to equal the effect of two aspirin (Wild 1994). Unfortunately, this substance has been advertised as aspirin free, giving the impression that it does not have the same side effects as aspirin, like stroke, stomach irritation, and Reye's syndrome in children.

Hormones

The two hormones naturally produced by the body, obtainable without prescription in this country, and receiving by far the most media attention regarding their claims and dangers are melatonin and DHEA (dehydroepiandrosterone). Both have been touted as miracle substances that are "Nature's age-reversing, disease fighting, sex enhancing hormone" (Pierpaoli and Regelson 1995) and the "Hormone from Heaven" whose role "in maintaining health is perhaps the greatest discovery of all time" (d'Raye 1995, p. 1). Let us explore the facts!

Melatonin

Melatonin is a hormone secreted principally at night by the pineal gland, which lies in the base of the brain. It is produced from serotonin, the substance that is manufactured from the amino acid tryptophan. Melatonin has progressively become more understood, and it is now clear that its main function is to regulate hormone secretion as pertains to sleep and wakefulness. Melatonin is secreted in darkness and is suppressed during light.

Melatonin levels have been found to be low in depressed individuals. Clinical trials have revealed, however, that low levels were due to antidepressant medication and other variables, as melatonin has not been effective in depression treatment and in some studies actually worsened the condition (Murray 1996). Melatonin has proven effective in the treatment of insomnia, but only when levels are low, as is common in the elderly and the depressed. There is much controversy regarding this hormone as experts such as Murray caution that melatonin can be effective as a sleep aid in small dosages. Nevertheless, it is a hormone and Murray advises professional counsel with its use.

Pierpaoli and Regelson, authors of *The Melatonin Miracle* (1995), believe that their research and that of others confirm the hormone's positive effect on the immune system, and as a cancer fighter, heart protector, stress reliever, and sex enhancer. They recommend regular supplements depending on age, beginning with 0.5 to 1 mg at bedtime for people ages 40 to 44 to a high of 3.5 to 5 mg at age 75 plus.

Physicians Irina Zhdanova and Richard Wurtman of MIT's Clinical Research Center have been conducting research on doses of 0.3 mg of melatonin, as MIT holds a patent on the use of low-dose melatonin along with Interneuron Pharmaceuticals, a company where both physicians are consultants. These researchers contend that 0.3 mg is equivalent to the levels found in young adults, which persist for 6 to 8 hours after ingestion. They also believe that, contrary to Regelson and Pierpaoli, older people may require less melatonin rather than more because their livers metabolize this hormone at a much slower pace. Additionally, the MIT researchers indicate that health food stores sell 3 mg tablets, which is ten times the amount that induces sleep. They estimate that such doses can cause drowsiness in the daytime and can also contribute to abnormal physiological rhythms, ultimately lowering body temperature and causing nightmares and night disorientation (Zhdanova and Wurtman 1996). It should be noted that the French, British, and Canadian governments have banned melatonin sales as there is not substantial evidence to indicate melatonin supplements are safe and reliable (University of California at Berkeley Wellness Letter 1996c).

It is safe to say that melatonin as a supplement should be taken judiciously and in small doses until more research is accumulated.

Dehydroepiandrosterone (DHEA)

This hormone has been compared to melatonin in terms of promise and controversy. DHEA has been stated to slow the aging process; eliminate stress; reverse obesity and increase muscle mass; prevent cancer, cardiovascular disease, Alzheimer's, bone loss, and diabetes; and increase overall well-being. DHEA is produced by the fetus, but production ends at birth until age 7, when it resumes. DHEA levels decrease after 30 years of age, and by age 60 levels are 5 to 15 percent of what they were at the highest production years. Levels are also reduced during illness. DHEA is sold in its precursor form as dioscorea, an herb derived from the Mexican yam. Researchers have found, however, that the body cannot transform a plant steroid into DHEA (University of California at Berkeley Wellness Letter 1996a).

In 1995, the New York Academy of Sciences sponsored a conference on DHEA that included many reports on experiments with DHEA and animals. These reports are considered questionable since the animals in question do not synthesize DHEA. Reviews summarized clinical evidence gathered by double-blind studies of DHEA with older adults. Studies reported volunteers having greater energy, increased ability to manage stress, and better quality of sleep. No change in sexual function was noted, nor was there any change in body fat content or glucose metabolism. These were small studies, and despite overall reports of a greater sense of well-being, presenters cautioned those with family histories of tumors responsive to hormones, like breast cancer or prostate cancer, to refrain from DHEA replacement therapy (New York Academy of Sciences 1995).

Studies by Elizabeth Barrett-Connor of the University of California at San Diego initially found that men with high DHEA levels had half the incidence of heart disease than men with low levels. Women, however, had higher risks of heart disease with high DHEA levels, and the men initially studied did not maintain positive results over time. It has also been demonstrated that people who are infected with HIV do not develop AIDS until their levels of DHEA drop. In England, 5,000 women were studied with breast cancer and they were found to have unusually low levels of DHEA. Additionally, mice who were bred to develop cancer remained without cancer when supplemented with DHEA (Walker 1994).

In terms of DHEA treatment of mice and rats who develop greater muscle tissue and reduce fat content, this has not been duplicated with human obese subjects. Bob Lefavi, Ph.D., assistant professor in Georgia Southern University's graduate health science program, reports (1996) that rats may be more sensitive to DHEA because they do not produce it naturally, akin to women's intense reaction to small amounts of testosterone. Lefavi encourages individuals to examine research, not marketing claims, when deciding to use supplements of any kind, similar to the active learner philosophy we discussed earlier. DHEA is being promoted by questionable practitioners and health manufacturers. It is too early, however, to jump on the bandwagon regarding this "Hormone from Heaven" that could send us there before our time.

ALTERNATIVE MEDICINE

In 1993 the *New England Journal of Medicine* published a study, often quoted by alternative practitioners, that reported that one in three adults in the United States stated that they had used an unconventional therapy and that more people had visited unconventional practitioners than primary care doctors. This study also found that in 1990, alternative health care, including supplements, books, and other associated products, produced a $13.7 billion business, with only $3 billion being paid by insurance coverage. The Office of Alternative Medicine was established in 1992 with a budget of $2 million and in 1995 it had been raised to $5.4 million. Alternative medicine is clearly gaining in popularity and is even being taught in a quarter of our conventional medical schools (Krajick 1996).

Robert Pelletier, author of the thought-provoking text, *Sound Mind, Sound Body: A New Model for Life Long*

Health (1994), calls for the integration of the best of allopathic and alternative medicine in the interest of designing the most complete health care system possible.

Allopathic or conventional Western medicine is very good at managing trauma, acute bacterial infections, medical and surgical emergencies, and other crises. It is very bad at managing viral infections, chronic degenerative disease, allergy and autoimmunity, many of the most serious kinds of cancer, mental illness, functional illness (a disturbance in the function of an organ in the absence of major physical or chemical changes), and those conditions in which the mind plays an active role in creating susceptibility to disease. It is not wise to seek allopathic care for a disease that conventional medicine cannot treat. it is not wise to resort to alternative practitioners when you have a disease that conventional medicine can treat very well. [p. 233]

In an article entitled "The Best of Both Worlds," internist Timothy McCall (1996) (author of *Examining Your Doctor: A Patient's Guide to Avoiding Harmful Medical Care*), comments on the 72 percent of individuals surveyed in the *New England Journal* study cited earlier who reported that they visited an alternative practitioner, but did not tell their physician for fear of ridicule. He encourages people to be frank, as it is important to prevent drug and herb interactions and prevent duplication of services. He also encourages people to expect openness of the part of the physician and to take advantage of

conventional methods that are preventive like mammo-
grams, pap smears, colon cancer screening, and vaccina-
tions for children. He recommends alternative therapies for
chronic ailments such as lower back pain and chronic pain,
and guided imagery for cancer patients undergoing chemo-
therapy to counter side effects. He additionally reminds the
reader, as we discovered in the section on herbs, that natural treatment does not necessarily equal safe treatment.

The following sections describe the major alternative
therapies being used by those seeking more natural means
of obtaining optimal health.

Naturopathy

Naturopathy is a form of alternative healing and health
that emphasizes the body's natural healing powers to
maintain and restore health. Naturopaths focus on disease-
preventing lifestyles and are experts in herbalism, nutrition, and homeopathy. They can perform minor surgeries
but cannot prescribe pharmaceutical drugs. A naturopath
is likely to treat an immune deficiency illness with vitamin and mineral supplements along with organic dietary
recommendations, rather than treating the symptoms
exclusively. A naturopathic physician is not oriented to
treating emergency and trauma cases, but is more of a
specialist in the treatment of chronic and degenerative
illnesses, as well as being expert in terms of teaching disease prevention. Their expertise usually involves herbal

medicine, homeopathy, acupuncture, herbal medicine, nutrition, hydrotherapy, and physical medicine (Goldberg 1993). In personal communication with naturopathic physician and Bastyr University graduate Jody Tonelli-Chapin, N.D., it became apparent that clients are now looking to naturopaths, with their new popularity, to prescribe regimens of supplements in the same manner that individuals have looked to allopathic physicians to prescribe magical medications with the hope of avoiding lifestyle changes. She emphasizes, however, that the naturopath is trained to understand causes of illness and to develop healing lifestyle changes rather than be the idealized guru who dispenses magic. The naturopath is a thoughtful practitioner who ultimately empowers each client to do his/her own treatment.

Naturopaths were licensed by half of the states in the United States in the 1930s, but declined to six states by the 1980s, reportedly due to protests by the American Medical Association. Utah and Maine recently passed legislation licensing naturopathic physicians and it is expected that more states will follow in the near future. The American Association of Naturopathic Physicians provides information by telephone (503-255-4860).

Osteopathy

Osteopathy is a school of healing founded by Andrew Taylor Still (1827–1917), who was dissatisfied with conventional medicine of his time and began the process of manipulating bones as a means of restoring balance to the body. Osteopaths today manipulate and palpate the muscles, bones, joints, spinal column, and nerves to correct structural imbalances and to allow the body to return to its natural ability to cure itself. Osteopathy is considered a form of physical medicine (when practiced conventionally) that primarily treats the musculoskeletal system through physical therapy, joint manipulation, and postural corrections. Osteopaths can essentially treat the same conditions as allopathic physicians, while being particularly effective with joint difficulties, chronic fatigue syndrome, arthritis, high blood pressure, heart disease, and nerve disorders (Goldberg 1993).

Osteopaths additionally provide counsel regarding nutrition, exercise, stress, and overall lifestyle. The University of New England, for instance, a well-regarded school of osteopathic medicine in the East, offers community residents comprehensive health programs for those targeted for major illness. These programs consist of nutritional and stress management advice as well as monitored exercise programs and osteopathic manipulating, if necessary. Osteopaths have a greater range of privilege than naturopaths in this country as they can prescribe pharmaceuticals and practice surgery and are more readily integrated into conventional medical circles. Information can be obtained from the American Osteopathic Association (800-621-1773).

Ayurveda

This is a 6,000-year-old system of natural health that is the traditional healing practice of India. *Ayurveda*, which means the science or knowledge of life, is a spiritual philosophy that is based on universal life energy called *prana*. This life force is affected by three forces called *vata* (air), *pitta* (fire), and *kapha* (water), which are believed to determine a person's body type, constitution, favorite foods, activities, and overall health. Practitioners of ayurveda use herbs, diet, acupuncture, and massage to balance the body and restore harmony. Ayurveda therapies that have drawn interest recently are the herbs ashwagandha and gugulipid, which have shown promising results in treating fertility problems and high cholesterol, respectively. This form of healing is not a licensed medical practice in this country, unlike osteopathy and naturopathy, and is generally practiced by lay people for holistic health purposes.

Homeopathy

This is a form of alternative medicine founded by Samuel Hahnemann, a German physician who believed that a patient's symptoms should be treated with microdoses of the same substance that would produce these symptoms in a healthy person. The homeopath typically prescribes tiny pellets that have been made from diluted herbs, minerals, or animal substances. An example is the use of Arnica (mountain daisy) as a treatment utilized by marathon runners for relieving muscle aches, cramping, and swelling.

Hahnemann's famous conceptualization, established by ancient philosophers, is the law of similars, which states that like cures like. This construct is opposite to allopathic or conventional medicine where medications are prescribed that have no relationship to the symptoms being treated. An allopathic physician, for example, would prescribe an antihistamine to treat the symptoms of hay fever, while a homeopath would prescribe a microdose of the substance that would produce symptoms in larger quantities to bolster the body's defense system against the pathogen. One approach is an attempt to eliminate symptoms, while the other is an attempt to eliminate the cause. The reader is cautioned regarding the recent proliferation of homeopathic products being touted by drug chains and pharmacists, as these substances are not standardized and make claims that tend to be extreme. The homeopath is noted for spending considerable time determining the unique formula to treat any given individual's problems, whereas the substances being advertised are not tailored to the individual, but are rather general mixes of substances purported to accomplish many unsubstantiated aims. Information can be obtained from the National Center of Homeopathy (703-548-7790).

Chiropractic

Daniel Palmer (1845–1913) founded chiropractic medicine as an attempt to counteract the harsh drug therapies of his day. He used body work and spine manipulation as a means to treat many diseases. Chiropractors basically manipulate the spine to correct misalignments that are thought to cause illnesses throughout the body. These misalignments are called sublaxations and properly restored alignment theoretically returns the neuromuscular system to equilibrium. Chiropractors are usually divided into two general groups, those who practice through locating sublaxations and removing them and those who are labeled mixers. Mixers also use other natural therapies to relieve pain and promote health, such as electrical stimulation, massage exercise, and nutrition. Research has revealed that chiropractic treatments are quite effective with lower back pain and, recently, some promise has been found with removing sublaxations in the nervous system of those suffering from chemical dependencies. These treatments have resulted in individuals increasing their probability of completing drug programs (Goldberg 1993). In training for the 100th Boston Marathon, I developed mid-back pain of significant proportions. I had several chiropractic treatments with a chiropractor, Denise Henson-Brosler, that lessened the pain significantly and allowed me to run the marathon pain free. Dr. Henson-

Brosler uses a gentle manipulation technique in contrast to other practitioners who may aggressively adjust. This gentler approach is recommended, as more force did not seem necessary or appealing. In my case, the pain has returned in this year's training and may need renewed treatments.

Chiropractors are licensed in all fifty states, although there is significant variance; some chiropractors practice exclusively by manipulation of the spine. Fifteen million individuals sought chiropractic help in the last year. Information can be obtained by calling the American Chiropractic Association (703-276-8800).

Acupuncture

Acupuncture has been heralded as providing treatment to more people than any other form of complete medicine. Traditional Chinese medicine (TCM), essentially the healing model of acupuncture, shiatsu (body work), herbalism, and tai chi (healing movement), has been brought to the West by practitioners from China, Korea, Japan, and Vietnam through texts and direct teachings of masters of this medical system. Acupuncture is considered a preventive art rather than primarily curative. Practitioners in China are viewed with less esteem if they have to practice curatively as compared to those masters who could successfully prevent illness through their counsel, and secondarily through intervention and medications (Golan 1995).

Acupuncture is based on the belief that health is determined by maintaining a balanced flow of energy throughout the body. This energy, called *qi*, moves in the body along twelve principal pathways called meridians. Each meridian is thought to be associated to organs such as the lung, liver, and kidneys, as well as specific areas of the body. An initial acupuncture consultation consists of the acupuncturist taking a medical history, observing the color of the tongue and the face. Examination of the wrist is used to determine information gleaned through twelve radial pulses considered significant in Chinese medicine. Upon completing the medical history and testing the pulse, needles are usually placed in several locations, with fewer needles used by the most skilled acupuncturist. Acupuncture is generally without pain; needles are usually presterilized and disposable. Treatments can vary in length, and occasionally needles are left in the patient beyond the time spent with the acupuncturist. Bruce Pomeranz, a physiologist from the University of Toronto, has published thirty-nine papers on acupuncture and pain. He has concluded, through many experiments where he has placed needles into false points (not recognized by Chinese charts), that endorphins and cortisol, a hormone with anti-inflammatory propensities, are activated when acupuncture points are stimulated by needles (Foreman 1995a). These findings may relate to the reports of psychiatrist James Gordon, chair of an advisory council to the

National Institutes of Health's Office of Alternative Medicine. Gordon, an advocate of holistic psychiatry, was recently featured in an article in *Health* magazine entitled, "Treat the Body, Heal the Mind" (Carlin 1997). Gordon describes how psychotherapy treatment is enhanced by alternative methods, most notably acupuncture. He places acupuncture needles in the feet, ankles, and trunk of a patient, instructing her to focus on deep breathing while he leaves the consulting room for a half hour. He returns and initiates talk therapy, with the patient reporting an increased ability to express depth of emotion. This particular patient was not able to reach this level of intensity with traditional psychotherapy and antidepressant regimes. Gordon's protocol then calls for additional adjunct support through meditation, exercise, dietary changes, herbal supplements, acupuncture treatments, and psychotherapy.

The World Health Organization has reported that acupuncture can treat 104 conditions, including bursitis, tendonitis, asthma, addictions, migraine, and tension headaches, as well as several other nonemergency conditions (Goldberg 1993). It has been estimated that Americans make 9 to 12 million visits to acupuncturists a year. There have been over 200 randomized controlled studies performed on the effectiveness of acupuncture for various concerns, but the methodology has been traditionally poor, rendering conflicting results (Foreman 1995a). Several studies establish the effectiveness of acupuncture with addictions, for instance, citing that the United States House of Representatives and the Senate Appropriations Committee declared that acupuncture for substance abuse is not only successful, but also cost-effective. On the other hand, a number of studies have found that acupuncture for the treatment of smoking, drinking, and drug abuse is no more effective than other abstinence therapies. It has been consistently indicated, however, that acupuncture is well received because it is pain free, easy to administer, and causes few side effects (Cui 1995, Worner et al. 1992).

In an effort to experience this process firsthand, I recently had an acupuncture treatment with a licensed acupuncturist and herbalist, Louis Pearl, L. Ac. The insertion of needles was painless and the relaxation induced was, in my experience, akin to a deep meditative state. It was also clear that many variables were at work, with the manner of the acupuncturist a key factor. I have found that alternative practitioners tend to be kind, compassionate, and calming, which has been a consistent finding with acupuncturists regardless of whether their treatment goal is reached. Information can be obtained by calling the American Association of Acupuncture and Oriental Medicine (919-787-5181).

Yoga/Meditation

The ancient practices of meditation and yoga have gained popularity in this country and throughout Europe since masters from India became known to the West during the 1960s. Meditation is the practice of training the mind to be aware of the moment, the life force of the breath, and the resultant stillness of deep tranquility. It is thought to be the opposite of automatic thinking clouded by the constant bombardment of stimuli around us. It is generally classified as either concentrative or mindfulness meditation.

Concentrative meditation is associated with focusing on a mantra (a sound), an image, or one's own breath. Mindfulness meditation focuses on the entirety of experience—thoughts, sensations, feelings—without particular involvement in any aspect of experience. This form is akin to watching objects pass by in a flowing current without focus on any one item, but with heightened awareness of the overall experience. These meditative methods are designed to improve one's ability to calm the mind and to learn how to limit the reactiveness of the mind, respectively (Goldberg 1993).

The complementary practice of yoga, a 5,000-year-old discipline, has similar psychological effects, as well as significantly improving stamina, coordination, and endurance. Most contemporary stretching exercises have their origins in yoga practice, with particular postures being helpful for an assortment of disorders. Positive results have been substantiated with back pain, arthritis, insomnia, menstrual problems, hypertension, heart disease, obesity, diabetes, alcoholism, and nicotine addictions (Goldberg 1993).

Herbert Benson, father of the relaxation response, has demonstrated in his thirty years of research that both yoga and transcendental meditation decrease oxygen consumption, respiratory rate, heart rate, and blood pressure while increasing alpha waves (electric current from the cerebral cortex, considered a relaxed state in normal, healthy adults) (Goleman 1993). The benefits of yoga and meditation are not, for the most part, controversial, as with some other alternative or complementary practices. There is widespread agreement as to the positive effects of both practices in the mind–body literature. Stress reduction programs are now plentiful in hospitals, covered by insurers, and standardly based in various forms of meditation and yoga practice. The reader is referred to the International Association of Yoga Therapists (415-383-4587) for information about the various forms and schools of yoga, and to the Institute of Transpersonal Psychology (415-327-2006) for information on various forms of meditation and research.

Spirituality

The field of behavioral medicine has been far from charitable to those who believe in the power of prayer and the peace of mind obtained from believing in a particular religious philosophy. Freud basically understood religion to be a defense against man's fear of mortality, a view that is again being echoed by those who in fact believe in the positive aspects of prayer for health reasons, but are not necessarily advocates of religious belief.

Herbert Benson, cited above for his classic *Relaxation Response* and of the recently released *Timeless Healing* (1996), believes that humans are genetically programmed for believing in a higher power. Benson arrived at this discovery as he studied meditators who believe in a higher power. He determined that those with such conviction obtained a higher degree of health than those who practiced his relaxation response but had no such religious experience. His supposition is that prayer operates neurochemically, similarly to meditation, affecting corticosteroids (stress hormones) and thus influencing the immune system and, ultimately, providing defense against disease. Other researchers have established that prayer and meditation are controlled by the amygdala, a part of the brain's limbic system that regulates emotion, sexuality, and depthful memories (Wallis 1996). Neuroscientist Bessel van der Kolk of Massachusetts General Hospital discovered, through use of positron emission tomography (PET) scans, that as trauma victims recall abuse memories, blood flow to the amygdala increases.

It appears that brain chemistry can substantiate the benefits of prayer and prayer has been attributed to many overall health benefits as well. In a recent article by Benson and Stark in *Natural Health* (1996) they cite the extensive research of Jeffrey Levin of Eastern Virginia Medical School, who reviewed "hundreds of epidemiologic studies and concluded that belief in God lowers death rates and increases health" (p. 75). He further comments on the authors of *Faith Factors* (Matthews and Larson 1994) as their collective study found that "religious factors are associated with increased survival; reduced anxiety, depression, and anger; reduced blood pressure; and improved quality of life for patients with cancer and heart disease" (Benson and Stark 1996, p. 75). What may be disheartening to some, however, is that Benson concludes that belief is essentially dictated by our fear of mortality and we are thus programmed to counter this anxiety, similar to Freud's early contention, through the genetic mechanism that allows prayer to soothe our fears and protect us from being devastated by the reality and finality of death.

Kenneth Cooper, also cited above for his books and work in the areas of aerobics and antioxidants, has recently written a text, *It's Better to Believe* (1995). He cites numerous research data that has found that those who believe are less prone to depression, smoking, and alcoholism, and are more likely to be free of cancer and coronary disease. He reports that research has confirmed that stress levels are lower among believers who have deep spiritual commitment. Cooper accents his own spiritual awakening in his writing, highlighting the interplay between spirituality, exercise, and nutrition. He differs from Benson's account in that he is clearly a believer himself, and he describes, in a comprehensive manner, how a belief system is central to good quality of life. It is interesting to note that both Cooper and Benson have been two of the rare physicians involved in holistic health since the 1960s. Both are widely respected and both have gravitated to the world of spirituality and prayer as their careers evolve and their longevity becomes more of an issue. Benson remains the committed researcher, as Cooper reaffirms deep spiritual convictions that maintained his sense of self throughout his early life. One view emphasizes the functional benefits of prayer, while the other emphasizes a spiritual core from which a belief system is created that governs our most fundamental decisions. A person's choices regarding nutrition and whether or not to exercise can then be viewed as a product of one's spiritual beliefs about the body, mind, and soul.

If it is then apparent that spirituality is fundamentally beneficial and, given our current health crisis, is cost-effective and covered by managed care guidelines, are we to assume that spirituality is a figment of our neurochemistry, an evolutionary function that is profoundly practical? George Sheehan wrestled with this question in his recent book, *Going the Distance* (1996), as he approached the hour of his death. Sheehan examined the writings of William James and noted others as they approached their deaths, mentioning that 95 percent of Americans report they believe in God but rarely address the subject in public. "Religion has been the cause of more rancor and strife than anything other than sex and money. We have learned to be wary about broaching the subject even with close friends" (p. 160). He decides that religion is a private matter, between oneself and one's interpretation of the Divine. He writes about his movement from needing an institutional church to constructing his own internal church by acquiring wisdom through experience. Sheehan settles on his view of Christ the athlete with a concentration on original splendor rather than original sin. He sees the athlete as symbolizing all we can become, all we have the potential to be. "One thing is certain. Whatever I do I must do with all my might, and do it with the unmistakable belief that pain and death are necessary, if I am to become the person I was meant to be on the day I was born" (pp. 166–167).

Spirituality, in its simplest sense, is becoming or realizing the potential within us. Some feel this potential has been given by God; others are not concerned with its origin, but are very concerned with its actualization. We are not destined to be addicts or to abuse ourselves or others, but to care for our health and to promote and facilitate balanced living in others. Perhaps living well creates an internal and external environment in which to die well.

ᘰ 6 ᘰ

Managed Care–
Quality Care

The advent of managed care has evoked enormous anxiety in the consumer and has produced similar reactiveness in medical practitioners. Some 38.6 million persons are now enrolled in managed care plans, which is a fourteen-fold increase of enrollment in the last five years (Ross and Weiser 1994). A recent literature analysis of managed care plans performance since 1980 was conducted by the Institute for Health and Aging of the University of California at San Francisco (Miller and Luft 1994):

> Compared with indemnity plans, health maintenance organizations plans had somewhat lower hospital admission rates, 1 to 20% shorter hospital length of stay, the same or more physician office visits per enrollee, less use of expen-

sive procedures and tests, greater use of preventive services, mixed results on outcomes, and somewhat lower enrollee satisfaction with services, but higher satisfaction with costs. The evidence does not support the hypothesis that prepaid group practice or staff model health maintenance organizations are more effective than individual practice association or network model health maintenance organizations. [p. 1512]

Although the authors caution that generalizations should be made carefully, these results do not seem farfetched and indicate a reality that both consumers and practitioners must adapt to and improve upon. Managed care plans cost less and probably provide less by accenting preventive care and restricting access to expensive procedures of no proven efficacy. It is not only the insurance industry that is driving these changes; it is America's corporations that are demanding accountability for their health care dollars, forming alliances like Massachusetts Healthcare Purchaser Group. This organization of twenty-seven corporate and government health care purchasers had data submitted on six clinical indicators by sixteen health plans. This resulted in valuable information provided to purchasers by allowing for comparative analysis among health plans (e.g., cesarean section rates), and it placed corporations in a position to submit data on the effectiveness of specific procedures (Jordan et al. 1995). The health care industry inevitably has the arduous task of reducing costs while providing high-level care, which means outcome analysis will be an ever-present part of the medical landscape, with corporate America assessing insurers and insurers accumulating databases that will establish ongoing protocols for treatment.

Psychotherapists have not been accustomed to being scrutinized and held accountable for the results of their efforts. The managed care reviewer and the clinician have often been at odds with each other, one seemingly trying to cut costs and the other seemingly trying to provide necessary treatment. At times and with certain companies of questionable credibility, this is the case, although not necessarily the norm. In June 1996 the American Psychological Association's practice directorate conducted an extensive survey of licensed psychologists to obtain an updated view of psychology practice (16,000 responses) in terms of work activity and professional concerns. Results indicated that psychotherapy hours occupied 43.9 percent of practitioners' time, with the next largest expenditure assessments (14 percent). Most licensed practitioners continue to work in solo practices (40 percent), 13 percent in medical settings, while 10 percent remained in academic and group practices, and 7 percent in government settings. The majority of psychologists continue to practice in a traditional manner, doing psychotherapy and assessments in solo practice. One-third of practitioners licensed since 1990 are in solo practice, but recent doctoral graduates with licenses are gravitating toward medical settings, more so than their older counterparts. Respondents overwhelmingly (80 percent) stated that managed care has had a negative impact on their professional work, 10 percent indicated no change, and 10 percent indicated that managed care had a positive impact. (This latter 10 percent is a curious finding.) Practitioners of recent licensure were more likely to use outcome measure, although the greatest predictor of outcome use was working in health care facilities rather than private practice, where requirements are less stringent.

Although the above survey is exclusive to psychologists, it is likely representative of other disciplines that bill privately for services, such as social work, psychiatry, and, in some states, mental health counselors. The impact of reduction of fees by managed care companies, coupled with an additional time requirement for review procedures and outcome measures, can affect one's practice dramatically. How one copes with these pressures, however, is potentially grounds for positive change and growth among practitioners, their patients, and the health care system itself.

This book has discussed the interactional origins of distress and, counteractively, their interactional remedies (empathy, interactional balance, tension management, internalization, and interpretation). We have also discussed the group therapist's commitment to understanding the interplay between cultural change and the individual, with our unending attempts to identify the relational ingredients that lead some to adapt and at times welcome change, as contrasted to those who seem to fall apart in the face of perceived newness and dissimilarity. Our ability to effectively negotiate with the managed care entity is thus an interpersonal opportunity to display balanced management of ambivalence, frustration, and anger. It is an opportunity to display how to cope with change and succeed, rather than withdraw from, or impulsively attack, a negative force. The psychotherapist must lead the way in terms of accommodating to our fast-paced world where change is a given. The therapist must lead the way in negotiating fairness in fees, coverage, and mutual respect between two parties. A credible managed care reviewer who denies additional sessions based on a reasonable interpretation of the medical necessity clause, which is clearly indicated in the patient's insurance brochure, is not re-creating childhood abuse even though it is understandable how a patient may confuse historical and present-day reality. On the other hand, a reviewer who arbitrarily denies sessions with no reasonable clinical explanation, even though the insurance brochure is clearly misleading in terms of patient visits, should be dealt with firmly and with adherence to the facts. We are no longer removed from the real-world process of interpersonal intensity; the affect is in the room, and, as in the group therapy environment, the opportunities abound. The therapist, akin to the parent aiding a child in interpersonal resolution, has a joint problem to solve with the patient. We must, particularly with character-damaged individuals, give the patient access to our ability to reason and to manage impulses, and to our internal sense of integrity that is the basis of our interpersonal balance and internal cohesion in the face of conflict.

It is common to question whether healing is possible in the current health care system where patients tend to feel that obtaining health care is more of a business transaction than an effort at forming therapeutic relationships that enhance healing (Noble 1995). The psychotherapist, more than any other practitioner, is in a position to provide these relationships; the requirements are more rigorous, but they also bear greater reward for patient and therapist alike.

Therapists realize that costs must be curtailed. How much of a reduction is fair? There is significant variation among insurers in terms of reasonable remuneration, session allowance given specific diagnostic problems, and equity in terms of payment timeliness. Some insurers cut rates drastically while their profit margins increase; session approvals are meager and require paperwork that is both unnecessary and redundant. Others, which tend to be the norm, conduct reviews in clinically meaningful ways, grant what they advertise, pay an equitable fee, and reward the practitioner through direct referrals as positive treatment outcomes are recognized and validated. Reviewers of credible organizations tend to value clinicians who give honest evaluations, can quickly assess diagnostically, and keep patients from utilizing expensive hospital benefits.

Hospitalization is frequently monitored. Clinicians who have traditionally used hospitals to manage character disorders and addictive disorders, particularly during treatment impasses, now find managed care criteria prohibitive in this regard. Some therapists view hospital admissions as a hindrance to treatment. The ability to manage intense interactions with patients with balance and thoughtfulness is most important and grossly underestimated in terms of its complexity. To tolerate and facilitate such interactions the psychotherapist must respond empathically, without sadistic intent, to the onslaught of projected criticism, which is usually forthcoming from character-disordered patients. These interactions challenge the therapist's own character structure and often reveal unresolved narcissistic wounds through the therapist's experience of the patient's projected aggression. The ability to therapeutically respond and understand these dynamics without the hindrance of countertransference is key to the success of treatments. However, hospitalization is appropriate for psychotic patients with severe medication complications, severe major depression with acute suicidal threat, addictive disorders requiring medical stabilization as in the case of eating disorders, and some alcoholics, substance abusers, and misdiagnosed dual-diagnosis patients. But transference complications with pronounced character-disordered patients are not a valid reason for hospitalization.

L. W. Hays (1995), chief psychologist at Prairie View Hospital in Kansas, administered a battery of psychological tests to psychiatric inpatients within 24 hours after admission, prior to discharge, and at 1, 3, and 12 months postdischarge. He found that personality type influences reactions to various treatment modalities during short hospitalizations, influences perceptions of the treatment environment, and alters patient perceptions at discharge and thereafter. Characterologically disturbed individuals were likely to report that they did not receive the help they needed, despite remaining in the hospital two days longer than others and using more resources. They had high recidivism rates, leading Hays to conclude that short-term hospital stays for these individuals are not successful or cost-effective.

Outcome measures are widely used in the managed care environment. The newsletter *Psychotherapy Finances* (April 1996) recently reported that hundreds of outcome measurements are currently being used, although twenty-four behavioral health care tools are most often those of choice, with the Addiction Severity Index (ASI), Behavioral and Symptom ID Scale (Basis-32), the Client Satisfaction Questionnaire (CSQ), and the Global Assessment of Functioning (GAF) the most frequently utilized. Rapid assessment instruments (RAIs) are generally considered useful in that they are efficient (easy to use), low cost, and assessable (they provide information that is initially hard to observe). They provide disclosure of information that a patient may feel inhibited to reveal at first (e.g., sexual satisfaction inventories), and they offer comparability in that they can be contrasted with established standard norms or a patient's former results. Some RAIs offer neutrality in that they are constructed without adherence to any particular theoretical position, whereas others are theoretically biased. An additional disadvantage is found if clinicians employ RAIs in place of comprehensive evaluations, for these instruments cannot take the place of methodical, ongoing psychotherapy, which slowly reveals origins of problems and remedies disturbances. Brief measures tend to measure generalities, not provide awareness of the subtleties of complex disorders. They should be viewed as tools that function as gross aids to treatment. Information from RAIs should be examined carefully and weighed with other relevant clinical data before any decisions regarding treatment are made. Self-report is flawed when financial interests are involved, either for the patient's benefit when additional sessions or hospital days are required, or with therapists administering instruments to their own psychotherapy patients where additional payments are needed. Case-mix variables must be controlled as well as honest intent established, so that validity can be maintained and these instruments can be useful (Corcoran and Fisher 1987).

In conclusion, managed care is a reality to be dealt with, not something to be denied or avoided, or become an entanglement between patient and therapist resulting in a negative treatment outcome. People come to psychotherapy seeking to gain strength and the skill to effectively manage their lives. Regardless of how painful it can be, individuals are willing to commit to the often arduous process of intensive psychotherapy as they come to realize that the pain of avoidance is greater than the time-limited pain of treatment that eventually leads to resolution of conflict. Psychotherapists must help patients deal with the actualities of their lives, including the changing landscape of their health care. We must maintain our own integrity through joining credible managed care panels that require us to reduce fees modestly in exchange for direct referrals and treatment plans based on sound clinical protocols. Inevitably, good treatment reduces costs and provides for patient satisfaction.

It is also necessary to explain to patients the criteria for compliance with medical necessity insurance clauses, and the differentiation between this necessity and personal growth treatment, which is not acute but clearly desirable to many as a quality of life enhancer. If patients are dealt with honestly, effectively, and with caring from the outset, they may continue in therapy beyond the phase for which coverage is provided (medically necessary treatment) to achieve more comprehensive gains (personal growth). Fee arrangements at that point are exclusively between patient and psychotherapist, and the interactional elements of equity are to be examined from both perspectives. The therapist's comfort or lack of comfort will become readily apparent to the patient as will other countertransference complications such as authority conflicts, rescue fantasies, boundary confusion, and unresolved regulation of masochistic and sadistic tendencies. The establishment of equitable fees is extremely revealing of both parties and offers a great opportunity for the understanding of relationships of reciprocity if managed properly. But even clear communication will result in some patients feeling abandoned and enraged by the limitations of the insurer, and ultimately the psychotherapist. These moments of emotional intensity must be dealt with directly, empathically, and with the interactional balance we have discussed, so that the patient is benefited by having the opportunity to internalize the therapist's ability to manage emotional depth without becoming overly permissive or detached. Psychotherapists cannot undo the patient's past, or change their financial and insurance situation. We can, however, facilitate a process by which individuals can learn to heal past wounds so that energy is free to address today's complicated challenges with hope, as potentials for growth previously hidden are uncovered.

⤳ 7 ⤲

Conclusion

This book has discussed the origins of abuse of self and others (masochism-sadism), the models of addiction, and a reconceptualized format of group psychotherapy used as a primary modality of treatment. This new model is ideally suited to addressing rapidly changing societal and relational pressures that often lead to pronounced alienation. We explored the contributions of interactional aspects of disorders and interactional elements to an effective healing process. We traced the therapeutic pathways that establish a solid sense of self in individuals as they release their attachment to unhealthy addictions and behaviors. They become active rather than passive learners. Individuals vary in their level of attainment of overall health, but it is nevertheless remarkable how those who have suffered tremendously for years can become invested in comprehensive health. The best results occur once a continuous realistic regard for oneself has been established. With a stable sense of self, anxiety and impulses are managed and competent self-direction and a desire for further growth allow new challenges and new learning to be integrated into an ever-expanding self.

Recent advances in object relations theory and self psychology have moved classical psychoanalytic theory from an instinctual, libidinal focus to a focus on the dynamics of interpersonal relationships. Social systems theory advanced psychological inquiry further toward a holistic perspective, which includes an emphasis on the intrapsychic and the interpersonal, as well as considering the group interactive influence on the behavior of the individual. The group model detailed in the therapeutic perspective section of Chapter 3 integrates the best of these models with interactive group therapy modalities and clinical experience.

The behavioral medicine literature has featured several articles calling for treatment to be focused on the whole person rather than on selective objective measures of health that are independent of life events. Noble (1995) raised the question of whether healing is possible in the current health system. Patients tend to feel that obtaining health care is more of a business transaction than an effort to facilitate a therapeutic relationship to enhance health. Other authors, such as Poggenpoel (1994), call for multidimensional treatment of depression and other disturbances. That holistic perspective allows for optimal healing since the patient feels tended to in a comprehensive manner. Zigmund (1995) examines the limitations of medicine, and attempts to broaden the traditional biomedical approach by emphasizing the expansive advantage of the biopsychosocial model of diseases. He concludes that medicine is not merely a science but also an art that can help immeasurably when interactions between caregiver and patient are maximized.

The emphasis of the biopsychosocial model is akin to an emphasis on holism in that both conceptualizations represent an attempt to view individuals in their entirety rather than through a narrow lens. Mim Landry states that one of the most important breakthroughs in the field of addiction treatment is the awareness that addiction is a biopsychosocial disease.

It is hoped that readers have gained further insight into the process by which suffering individuals move from narrow self-perspectives to a holistic view of themselves that results in better health and a renewed purpose in life. The medium of group psychotherapy is ideal for developing wholeness, as one's fixed views of oneself and others are examined in a way that leads to a "big picture" perspective.

My favorite movie, *It's a Wonderful Life*, is reminiscent of this perspective as George Bailey, played by Jimmy Stewart, moves from the narrow perspective of his suffering to the expansive, holistic view of the totality of his life with the aid of an angel, who provides a vivid account of the effects of Mr. Bailey's life on others. Frank Capra, the director, evidently understood something about the meaning and resultant joy experienced when one moves from a singular focus on oneself to the heights of one's entire experience.

The past two decades of clinical practice have provided exciting opportunities for experiencing advancing psychological theories that have accommodated cultural change. Patients seeking psychotherapy are usually suffering from some form of relational difficulty, whether this manifests itself through isolation, abuse, or undue aggression directed to the self or others. Unlike in Freud's era, when internal conflicts in wishes and impulses were the focus fueled by inherently problematic Victorian norms, our cultural acceptance and expression today are vastly different. Our problems are more clearly related to the dissolution of the family, community, place of worship, and other agencies that have provided solid relational grounding in the past.

Many clients today have multiple presenting problems. Managed care facilities must balance effective care with cost analysis. Clients need to have a strong alliance with the care provider and clear expectations to move from acute, medically necessary care toward elective supportive care.

The health impact designed in this book uses the best

of individual therapies and group interaction therapies to build the sense of self in clients. As this is secured, educative and experiential training in a spectrum of holistic techniques is added so the client can maintain his or her gains and continue to work toward stable self-care.

Theoretical developments need to parallel cultural change as we move from internal concerns to interactional needs and beyond. The holistic perspective is in harmony with the emotional and psychological longings of our time. An understanding of the "big picture" allows for the experience of meaning in one's life rather than a sense of alienation. In a changing world an integrated whole is a necessity.

This model emphasizes holism and the treatment of the emotional, biological, psychological, spiritual, and interactional elements. To cope with the changing structure of health care provision and the increasing demands of multiple or severely afflicted clients suffering from addictions or abuse or both, we need clear, clinically effective guidelines to use individual, group, and holistic modalities in a combination that maximizes the impact for outpatient support. The model of care presented is applicable to our current health care challenges. It is hoped that our understanding of how new strategies for sustained, cost-effective outpatient treatment in managed care settings using individual, group, and holistic modalities can be further enhanced. Our quest for balanced living and balanced relating is dependent on our efforts.

References

Allen, S. N., and Bloom, S. L. (1994). Group and family treatment of post-traumatic stress disorder. *Psychiatric Clinics of North America* 17(2):425–437.

American Psychological Association. (1994). Toward a new psychology of men. *American Psychological Association Monitor* 25(9):1, 40–41.

American Psychological Association Practice Directorate. (1996). *Practitioner Survey Results Offer Comprehensive View of Psychology Practice* 4(2):1–5, June.

Applegate, L. (1996). Nutrition: performance on demand. *Runners World*, June, pp. 30–32.

Arieti, S. (1974). *Interpretation of Schizophrenia*. New York: Robert Bruner.

Arnot, R. (1996). Mind-altering protein. *Men's Journal*, June, pp. 101–104.

Aronson, J. K. (1993). *Insights in the Dynamic Psychotherapy of Anorexia and Bulimia*. Northvale, NJ: Jason Aronson.

Bailey, C. (1994). *Smart Exercise*. New York: Houghton Mifflin.

Balch, B., and Balch, B. (1990). *Prescription for Nutritional Healing*. New York: Avery Publishing Group.

Bass, A. (1995). Stress early in life may leave imprint for violence. *Boston Globe*, October 16, pp. 29–32.

——— (1996a). Alcoholism as disease: view comes into question. *Boston Globe*, April 9, pp. 1–6.

——— (1996b). Hidden memories. *Boston Globe*, March 18, pp. 25–27.

Bastiani, A. M., Rao, R., Weltzin, T., and Kaye, W. H. (1995). Perfectionism and anorexia nervosa. *International Journal of Eating Disorders* 17(2):147–152.

Beasley, J. (1989). *How to Defeat Alcoholism*. New York: Times Books.

Becker, R. J., and Kolit, M. Q. (1980). *Curative Aspects in Hospital Group Psychotherapy*. Unpublished manuscript.

Beeferman, D., and Orvaschel, H. (1994). Group psychotherapy for depressed adolescents: a critical review. *International Journal of Group Psychotherapy* 44(4):463–475.

Benson, H. (1996). *Timeless Healing*. New York: Scribners.

Benson, H., and Stark, M. (1996). Reason to believe. *Natural Health*, June, pp. 72–76.

Berger, M., Berger, L., Sager, C., and Kaplan, H. S., eds. (1972). Psychogeriatric group approaches. *Progress in Group and Family Therapy*. New York: Brunner/Mazel.

Berland, D., and Poggi, R. (1979). Expressive group psychotherapy with the aging. *International Journal of Group Psychotherapy* 29:87–109.

Bernfield, G., Clark, L., and Parker, C. (1984). The process of adolescent group psychotherapy. *International Journal of Group Psychotherapy* 34:111–126.

Betcher, R. W. (1983). The treatment of depression in brief inpatient group psychotherapy. *International Journal of Group Psychotherapy* 33:365–385.

Betcher, R. W., Rice, C. A., and Weir, D. M. (1982). The regressed inpatient group in a graded group treatment program. *American Journal of Psychotherapy* 36:229–239.

Blume, S. B. (1978). Group psychotherapy in the treatment of alcoholism. In *Practical Approaches to Alcoholism Psychotherapy*, ed. S. Zimberg, J. Wallace, and S. B. Blume. New York: Plenum.

Brandes, N. S., and Moosbruger, L. (1985). A 15-year clinical review of combined adolescent young adult group therapy. *International Journal of Group Psychotherapy* 35:95–107.

Brownell, K., and Foreyt, J. (1986). *Handbook of Eating Disorders*. New York: Basic Books.

Bruch, H. (1962). Perceptual and conceptual disturbances in anorexia nervosa. *Psychosomatic Medicine* 24:187–199.

Buchele, B. C. (1994). Innovative uses of psychodynamic group psychotherapy. *Bulletin of the Menninger Clinic* 58(2):215–223.

Burfoot, A., and Post, M. (1996). Tight fitting genes. *Runners World*, June, p. 19.

Carlin, P. (1997). Treat the body, heal the mind. *Health Magazine*, January, pp. 73–78.

Carrion, P. G., Swann, A., Kellert, C. H., and Barber, M. (1993). Compliance with clinic attendance by outpatients with schizophrenia. *Hospital and Community Psychiatry* 44(8): 764–767.

Center for the Study of Anorexia and Bulimia. (1984). *Group*

Psychotherapy with Bulimia (Pamphlet). 1 West 91 St., New York, NY 10024.

Chaitow, L. (1985). *Amino Acids in Therapy*. London: Thorsons Publishing Group.

Chessick, R. (1977). *Intensive Psychotherapy of the Borderline Patient*. New York: Jason Aronson.

—— (1985). *Psychology of the Self and the Treatment of Narcissism*. Northvale, NJ: Jason Aronson.

Clark, W. G., and Vorst, V. R. (1994). Group therapy with chronically depressed geriatric patients. *Journal of Psychosocial Nursing and Mental Health Services* 32(5):9–13.

Cooper, D. E. (1981). Group psychotherapy with the elderly: dealing with loss and death. *American Journal of Psychotherapy* 38:203–214.

Cooper, K. (1989). *Preventing Osteoporosis*. New York: Bantam Books.

—— (1994). *Antioxidant Revolution*. Nashville: Thomas Nelson.

—— (1995). *It's Better to Believe*. Nashville: Thomas Nelson.

Corcoran, K., and Fisher, J. (1987). *Measures for Clinical Practice*. New York: Free Press.

Cui, M. (1995). Advances in studies on acupuncture abstinence. *Journal of Traditional Chinese Medicine* 15(4):301–307.

Debane, E. G., and DeCarufel, F. (1993). The context of transference interpretations in analytical group psychotherapy. *American Journal of Psychotherapy* 47(4):540–553.

deGroot, J. M., Kennedy, S., Rodin, G., and McVey, G. (1992). Correlates of sexual abuse in women with anorexia nervosa and bulimia nervosa. *Canadian Journal of Psychiatry* 37(7): 516–518.

Dies, R. R., and Teleska, P. A. (1985). Negative outcome in group psychotherapy. In *Negative Outcome in Psychotherapy and What to do About it*, ed. D. Mays and C. M. Franks. New York: Springer.

——— (1993). Research on group psychotherapy: overview and clinical applications. In *Group Therapy in Clinical Practice*, ed. A. Alonso and H. I. Swiller, pp. 473–518. Washington, DC: American Psychiatric Press.

Dobkin, P. L., Tremblay, R. E., Desmarais-Gervais, L., and Depelteau, L. (1994). Is having an alcoholic father hazardous for children's physical health? *Addiction* 89(12):1619–1627.

Dore, M. M., Doris, J. M., and Wright, P. (1995). Identifying substance abuse in maltreating families: a child welfare challenge. *Child Abuse and Neglect* 19(5):531–542.

Drake, R. E., McHugo, G. J., and Noordsy, D. L. (1993). Treatment of alcoholism among schizophrenic outpatients: 4 year outcomes. *American Journal of Psychiatry* 150(2):328–329.

d'Raye, T. (1995). *The Hormone from Heaven*. Keizer, OR: Hormones from Heaven etc.

Elbirik, K., Apprey, M., and Moles, K. (1994). Individual and group therapies as constructive continuous experiences. *American Journal of Psychotherapy* 48(1):141–154.

Emrick, C. D., and Silver, J. (1974). *Curative factors in hospital group psychotherapy*. Paper presented at the fifth annual meeting for the Society for Psychotherapy Research, Denver, CO, August.

Erdmann, R. (1989). *The Amino Revolution*. New York: Simon & Schuster.

Erickson, R. C. (1981). Small-group psychotherapy with patients on a short-stay ward: an opportunity for innovation. *Hospital and Community Psychiatry* 32:269–272.

Fain, J. (1996). Dr. Gilligan's prison education. *Boston Globe*, April 17, pp. 57–60.

Flores, P. J., and Mahon, L. (1993). The treatment of addiction in group psychotherapy. *International Journal of Group Psychotherapy* 43(2):143–156.

Foreman, J. (1995a). Meanwhile don't just sit there. *Boston Globe*, April 24, pp. 25–28.

——— (1995b). Any exercise is better than none. *Boston Globe*, October 31, pp. 28–29.

——— (1996a). Exercise appears to boost immune system to a point. Health Science, *Boston Globe*, January 1, pp. 45–46.

——— (1996b). Drink up or not? Studies in women are at odds on alcohol's risks and benefits, Health Science, *Boston Globe*, January 8, pp. 25–26.

——— (1996c). In medical labs, garlic is coming up roses. Health Science, *Boston Globe*, February 19, pp. 33–36.

——— (1996d). Study faults controlled drinking by alcoholics. Health Science, *Boston Globe*, March 13, pp. 1–12.

——— (1996e). Acupuncture: An ancient medicine is making its point. Health Science, *Boston Globe*, May 22, pp. 2–25.

Frank, J. O. (1975). Group therapy in the mental hospital. In *Group Psychotherapy and Group Function*, ed. M. Rosenbaum and Rev. M. M. Berger, pp. 465–482. New York: Basic Books.

Freud, S. (1896). Specific aetiology of hysteria. *Standard Edition* 3:163.

—— (1919). A child is being beaten. *Standard Edition* 17: 179–204.

—— (1921). Group psychology and the analysis of the ego. *Standard Edition* 18:67–134.

Frieling-Sonninber, W. (1995). Health is not just the absence of disease. *Pflege* (German), June, pp. 146–153.

Gans, J. S. (1990). Broaching and exploring the question of combined group and individual therapy. *International Journal of Group Psychotherapy* 40(2):123–137.

Gershoff, S. (1990). *Tufts University Guide to Total Nutrition.* New York: HarperCollins.

Getter, H., Litt, M. D., Kadden, R. M., and Cooney, N. L. (1992). Measuring treatment process in coping skills and interactional group therapies for alcoholism. *International Journal of Group Psychotherapy* 42(3):419–430.

Gilligan, J. (1996). *Violence: Our Deadly Epidemic and its Causes.* New York: Putnam.

Glick, R. A., and Myers, D. I. (1988). *Masochism: Current Psychoanalytic Perspectives.* Hillsdale, NJ: Analytic Press.

Golan, R. (1995). *Optimal Wellness.* New York: Ballantine Books.

Goldberg, B. (1993). *Alternative Medicine: The Definitive Guide.* Fife, WA: Future Medicine.

Goleman, D. (1993). *Mind/Body Medicine.* New York: Consumer Reports Books.

Goodsitt, D. (1985). Self-psychology and the treatment of anorexia nervosa. In *Handbook of Psychotherapy of Anorexia Nervosa and Bulimia*, ed. D. M. Garner and P. E. Garfinkel. New York: Guilford.

Greene, L. S., and Cole, M. D. (1991). Level and form of psychopathology and the structure of group therapy. *International Journal of Group Psychotherapy* 41(4):499–520.

Gruen, D. S. (1993). A group psychotherapy approach to post-partum depression. *International Journal of Group Psychotherapy* 43(2):191–203.

Gunderson, J. G. (1979). Individual psychotherapy. In *Disorders of Schizophrenic Syndrome*, ed. L. Bellak, pp. 364–398. New York: Basic Books.

Hall, A. (1985). Group psychotherapy for anorexia nervosa. In *Handbook for Psychotherapy of Anorexia Nervosa and Bulimia*, ed. D. M. Garner and P. E. Garfinkel. New York: Guilford.

Hall, S. S. (1997). Eat to fight cancer. *Health Science*, April, pp. 106–113.

Hamilton, J. D., Courville, T. J., Rechman, B., et al. (1993). Quality assessment and improvement in group psychotherapy. *American Journal of Psychiatry* 150(2):316–320.

Hannah, S. (1984a). Countertransference in inpatient group psychotherapy: implications for technique. *International Journal of Group Psychotherapy* 34:257–272.

——— (1984b). The words of the therapist: errors of commission and omission. *International Journal of Group Psychotherapy* 34:369–376.

Hays, L. W. (1995). Relating Psychological Testing to Prognosis and Outcomes. *Behavioral Health Management* 15(5): 21–25.

Helgeson, V. S. (1993). Implications of agency and communion for patients and spouse adjustment to a first coronary event. *Journal of Personality and Social Psychology* 64/5: 807–816.

Heller, R. F., and Heller, R. F. (1996). *Healthy for Life.* New York: Penguin Books.

Herbal roulette. (1995). *Consumer Reports,* November, pp. 698–705.

Herman, J. (1992). *Trauma and Recovery.* New York: Basic Books.

Hill, S. Y. (1995). Mental and physical health consequences of alcohol use in women. *Recent Developments in Alcoholism* 12:181–197.

Holderness, C. C., Brooks-Gunn, J., and Warren, M. P. (1994). Co-morbidity of eating disorders and substance abuse: review of the literature. *International Journal of Eating Disorders* 16(1):1–34.

Horner, A. J. (1979). *Object Relations and the Developing Ego in Therapy.* New York: Jason Aronson.

——— (1990). *The Primacy of Structure: Psychotherapy of Underlying Character Pathology.* Northvale, NJ: Jason Aronson.

Huebner, B. (1996). Burning cash not calories. *Boston Globe,* May 27, pp. 31–32.

Hughes, C., and Wells, M. (1991). Current conceptualizations on masochism: genesis and object relations. *American Journal of Psychotherapy* 14(1):53–69.

Hurst, A. G., and Gladieux, J. D. (1980). Guidelines for leading an adolescent group. In *Group and Family Therapy,* ed. L. R. Wolberg and M. L. Aronson. New York: Brunner/Mazel.

Johnson, D. R., Sandel, S., and Bruno, C. (1984). Effectiveness of different group structures for schizophrenic, character disordered, and normal groups. *International Journal of Group Psychotherapy* 34:415–429.

———— (1985). Expressive group psychotherapy with the elderly: a drama therapy approach. *International Journal of Group Psychotherapy* 35:109–127.

Jones, M. (1953). *The Therapeutic Community.* New York: Basic Books.

Jordan, H. S., Strauss, J. H., and Bailit, M. H. (1995). Reporting and using health plan performance information in Massachusetts. *Joint Commission Journal on Quality Improvement* 21(4):167–177.

Judge, M. G. (1993). Alcoholism's deadly sweet tooth. *Common Boundary* 11:53–56.

Kahn, E. M., and Kahn, E. W. (1992). Group treatment assignment for outpatients with schizophrenia: integrating recent clinical and research findings. *Community Mental Health Journal* 28(6):539–550; discussion 551–560.

Kahn, M. (1984). Group treatment intervention for schizophrenics. *International Journal of Group Psychotherapy* 34: 149–153.

Kanas, N. (1985). Inpatient and outpatient group therapy for schizophrenic patients. *American Journal of Psychotherapy* 34:431–439.

———— (1993). Group psychotherapy with bipolar patients: a review and synthesis. *International Journal of Group Psychotherapy* 43(3):321–333.

Kernberg, O. F. (1975). *Borderline Conditions and Pathological Narcissism.* New York: Jason Aronson.

———— (1976). *Object Relations Theory and Clinical Psychoanalysis.* New York: Jason Aronson.

———— (1980). *Internal World and External Reality.* New York: Jason Aronson.

Kibel, H. D. (1978). The rationale for the use of group psychotherapy for borderline patients in a short-term unit. *International Journal of Group Psychotherapy* 28:339–358.

—— (1981). A conceptual model for short-term inpatient group psychotherapy. *American Journal of Psychiatry* 138/1:74–80.

Kingston, L., and Prior, M. (1995). The development of patterns of stable, transient, and school-age onset aggressive behavior in young children. *Journal of the American Academy of Child and Adolescent Psychiatry* 34(3):348–358.

Kirman, J. H. (1995). Working with anger in groups: a modern analytic approach. *International Journal of Group Psychotherapy* 45(3):303–329.

Klein, K. H., ed. (1992). *Handbook of Contemporary Group Psychotherapy*, vol. 1. Madison CT: International Universities Press.

Klein, K. L., Orleans, J. F., and Soule, C. R. (1991). The axis 11 group: treating severely characterologically disturbed patients. *International Journal of Group Psychotherapy* 41:97–114.

Klein, R. H., Bernard, H. S., and Singer, D. L. (1992). *Handbook of Contemporary Group Psychotherapy*. Madison, CT: International Universities Press.

Kleinberg, J. L. (1995). Group treatment of adults in midlife. *International Journal of Group Psychotherapy* 45(2):207–222.

Klesges, R. C., Ray, J. W., and Klesges, L. M. (1994). Caffeinated coffee and tea intake and its relationship to cigarette smoking: an analysis of the second national health and nutrition examination survey (NHANES II). *Journal of Substance Abuse* 6(4):407–418.

Knapp, C. (1996). *Drinking: A Love Story*. New York: Dial.

Knowles, M., and Klevins, C. (1987). *Materials and Methods in Adult and Continuing Education*. Los Angeles: Klevins Publishers.

Knox, R. (1995). Only vigorous exercise found to lengthen life significantly. *Boston Globe*, April 19, p. 15.

Kohut, H. (1977). *The Restoration of the Self*. New York: International Universities Press.

———— (1980). Summarizing reflections. In *Advances in Self Psychology*, ed. A. Goldberg. New York: International Universities Press.

———— (1984). *How Does Analysis Cure?* Chicago: University of Chicago Press.

Krajick, K. (1996). Will the long life be a good life. *Natural Way Magazine*, August, pp. 45–47.

La Ban, M. M., Wilkins, J. C., Sackeyfio, A. H., and Taylor, R. S. (1995). Osteoporosis stress fractures in anorexia nervosa: etiology, diagnosis, and review of four cases. *Archives of Physical Medicine and Rehabilitation* 76(9):884–887.

Lacey, J. H. (1985). Time-limited individual and group treatment for bulimia. In *Handbook for Psychotherapy of Anorexia Nervosa and Bulimia*, ed. D. M. Garner and P. E. Garfinkel. New York: Guilford.

Landry, M. J. (1994). *Understanding Drugs of Abuse*. Washington, DC: American Psychiatric Press.

Langs, R. (1977). *The Therapeutic Interaction*. New York: Jason Aronson.

LaSalvia, T. A. (1993). Enhancing addiction treatment through psychoeducational groups. *Journal of Substance Abuse* 10(5):439–444.

LeFavi, R. (1996). Is this steroid-hormone the next miracle fat-loss pill? *Muscular Development. Fitness. Health*, August 8, pp. 175–206.

Leopold, H. S. (1976). Selective group approaches with psychotic patients in hospital settings. *American Journal of Psychotherapy* 30:95–102.

Leszcz, M., Feigenbaum, E., Sadavoy, J., and Robinson, A. (1985a). A men's group: psychotherapy for elderly men. *International Journal of Group Psychotherapy* 35:77–196.

Leszcz, M., Yalom, I. D., and Norden, M. (1985b). The value of inpatient group psychotherapy: patients' perception. *International Journal of Group Psychotherapy* 35:411–433.

Levin, J. D. (1987). *Treatment of Alcoholism and Other Addictions: A Self-Psychology Approach*. Northvale, NJ: Jason Aronson.

——— (1991). *Recovery from Alcoholism: Beyond Your Wildest Dreams*. Northvale, NJ: Jason Aronson.

——— (1995). *Introduction to Alcoholism Counseling*. Washington, DC: Taylor and Francis.

Lieberman, M. A., and Bliwise, N. G. (1985). Comparison among peer and professionally directed groups for the elderly: implications for the development of self-help groups. *International Journal of Group Psychotherapy* 33:21–39.

Marcovitz, R. J., and Smith, J. E. (1983). Patients' perceptions of curative factors in short-term group psychotherapy. *International Journal of Group Psychotherapy* 33:21–39.

Margen, S. (1995). *The New Wellness Encyclopedia.* New York: Houghton Mifflin.

Martin, C. S., Earleywine, M., Blackson, T. C., et al. (1994). Aggressivity, inattention, hyperactivity, and impulsivity in boys at high and low risk for substance abuse. *Journal of Abnormal Child Psychology* 22(2):177–203.

Matthews, D. A., and Larson, D. B. (1994). *Faith Factors.* John Templeton Foundation.

Maugars, Y., and Prost, A. (1994). Osteoporosis in anorexia nervosa. *Presse Medicale* 23(4):156–158.

Maxmen, J. S. (1973). Group therapy as viewed by hospitalized patients. *Archives of General Psychiatry* 28:404–408.

——— (1984). Helping patients survive theories: the practice of an educative model. *International Journal of Group Psychotherapy* 34:355–368.

McCall, T. (1996). The best of both worlds. *American Health Magazine*, April, p. 53.

Milam, J. R., and Ketcham, K. (1981). *Under the Influence.* Seattle, WA: Madorona Publishers.

Miller, R. H., and Luft, H. S. (1994). Managed care plan performance since 1980: a literature analysis. *Journal of the American Medical Association* 271(19):1512–1519.

Mitchell, J. E., Pyle, R. L., Pomeroy, C., et al. (1993). Cognitive-behavioral group psychotherapy of bulimia nervosa: importance of all variables. *International Journal of Eating Disorders* 14(3):277–287.

Mosher, L. R., and Gunderson, J. G. (1979). Group, family, milieu, and community support systems treatment of schizophrenia. In *Disorders of the Schizophrenic Syndrome*, ed. L. Bellak, pp. 399–452. New York: Basic Books.

Mosher, L. R., and Keith, S. J. (1980). Psychosocial treatment: individual, group, family, and community approaches. *Schizophrenia Bulletin* 6:10–41.

Moss, H., and Kirisci, L. (1995). Aggressivity in adolescent alcohol abusers: relationship with conduct disorder. *Alcoholism, Clinical and Experimental Research* 19(3):642–646.

Moss, V. A. (1991). Battered women and the myth of masochism. *Journal of Psychosocial Nursing and Mental Health Service* 29(7):18–23.

Murray, M. (1994). *Diabetes and Hypoglycemia.* Rocklin, CA: Prima Publishing.

—— (1996). *Natural Alternatives to Prozac.* New York: William Morrow.

National Institute on Alcohol Abuse (1990). *National Household Survey on Drug Abuse.* Rockville, MD: National Institute on Drug Abuse.

National Institutes of Health (1991). *Diagnosis and Treatment of Depression in Later Life.* Consensus Statement 1991: 9(3):1–27.

National Research Council (1993). Understanding and preventing violence. Washington, DC: National Academy Press.

New York Academy of Sciences (1995). DHEA and Aging, vol. 774. New York: Annals of New York Academy of Sciences.

Noble, M. A. (1995). The search for healing: Is it possible in contemporary health care? *Nursing Administration Quarterly* Spring:7–32.

Norris, J., and Kerr, K. L. (1993). Alcohol and violent pornography: responses to permissive and nonpermissive cues. *Journal of Studies on Alcohol: Supplement* 11:118–127.

Novick, J., and Novick, K. K. (1991). Some comments on masochism and the delusion of omnipotence from a developmental perspective. *Journal of the American Psychoanalytic Association* 39(2):307–331.

Ornstein, A. (1991). The dread to repeat: comments on the working-through process in psychoanalysis. *Journal of the American Psychoanalytic Association* 39(2):377–398.

Panken, S. (1983). *The Joy of Suffering: Psychoanalytic Theory and Therapy of Masochism.* New York: Jason Aronson.

Parloff, M. B., and Dies, R. R. (1977). Group psychotherapy outcome research, 1966–1975. *International Journal of Group Psychotherapy* 27:281–319.

Pelletier, K. (1994). *Sound Mind–Sound Body.* New York: Simon & Schuster.

Picker, L. (1996). Herbal medicine goes mainstream. *American Health Magazine*, May, pp. 70–75.

Pierpaoli, W., and Regelson, W. (1995). *The Melatonin Miracle.* New York: Pocket Books.

Pizzorno, J. (1996). *Total Wellness.* Rocklin, CA: Prima Publishing.

Poggenpoel, M. (1994). A holistic approach to depression. *Nursing RSA*, December, pp. 25–27.

Prino, C. T., and Peyrot, M. (1994). The effect of child physical abuse and neglect on aggressive, withdrawn, and prosocial behavior. *Child Abuse and Neglect* 18(10):871– 884.

Psychotherapy Finances. (1996). Outcomes: 24 behavioral health care outcome tools. 22(4):9–10.

Rachman, A. W., and Raubolt, R. P. (1984). The pioneers of adolescent group therapy. *International Journal of Group Psychotherapy* 34:387–413.

Rastman, M., Gillberg, I. C., and Gillberg, C. (1995). Anorexia nervosa 6 years after onset: part II. Cormorbid psychiatric problems. *Comprehensive Psychiatry* 36(1):70–76.

Riese, H., and Rutan, J. S. (1992). Group therapy for eating disorders: a step-wise approach. *Group* 16:79–83.

Romeo, F. (1994). Adolescent boys and anorexia nervosa. *Adolescence* 29(115):643–647.

Ross, B., and Weiser, M. A. (1994). Managed care: an opportunity for osteopathic physicians. *Journal of the American Osteopathic Association* 94(2):149–156.

Rowe, C. E., and Mac Isaac, D. S. (1991). *Empathic Attunement, The Technique of Psychoanalytic Self-Psychology.* Northvale, NJ: Jason Aronson.

Russakoff, M., and Oldham, J. M. (1984). Group psychotherapy and short-term treatment unit: an application of object relations theory. *International Journal of Group Psychotherapy* 34:339–354.

Scheidlinger, S. (1994). An overview of nine decades of group psychotherapy. *Hospital and Community Psychiatry* 45(3): 217–225.

Sege, I. (1996a). A therapist's demons: psychologist's memoir reveals her painful past as a patient. *Boston Globe*, March 28, pp. 85–90.

——— (1996b). Her time in a bottle: Caroline Knapp's memoir recounts her painful love affair with alcohol. *Boston Globe*, May 1, pp. 61–66.

Seppa, N. (1996). APA releases study on family violence. *APA Monitor*, April 1, p. 12.

Serok, S., Rabin, C., and Spitz, Y. (1984). Intensive gestalt group therapy with schizophrenics. *International Journal of Group Psychotherapy* 34:413–434.

Sheehan, G. (1996). *Going the Distance.* New York: Villard.

Shute, N. (1997). Aching for an arthritis cure. *U.S. News and World Report,* Health and Fitness, February, pp. 63–64.

Silbersiepe, K. A., and Hardy, A. (1995). Health habits of recovering alcoholics. *Maryland Medical Journal* 44(6):467–471.

Skodol, A. E., Oldham, J. M., Hyler, S. E., et al. (1993). Comorbidity of *DSM-III-R* eating disorders and personality disorders. *International Journal of Eating Disorders* 14(4): 403–416.

Slater, L. (1996). *Welcome to My Country.* New York: Random House.

Slavinsky-Holly, J. (1980). Treatment of the borderline in homogenous groups and the use of the "body transference technique." In *Group and Family Therapy,* ed. L. R. Walberg and M. L. Aronson. New York: Brunner/Mazel.

———— (1983). Combining individual and homogenous group psychotherapies for borderline conditions. *International Journal of Group Psychotherapy* 33:297–313.

———— (1988). *Borderline and Narcissistic Patients in Therapy.* Madison, CT: International Universities Press.

Sours, J. (1980). *Starving to Death in a Sea of Objects: The Anorexia Nervosa Syndrome.* New York: Jason Aronson.

Spotnitz, H. (1957). The borderline schizophrenic in group psychotherapy: the importance of individualization. *International Journal of Group Psychotherapy* 7:127–147.

Stotsky, B. A., and Zolik, E. S. (1965). Group psychotherapy with psychotics: 1921–1963: a review. *International Journal of Group Psychotherapy* 15:321–344.

Sugarman, A. (1991). Developmental antecedents of masochism: vignettes from the analysis of a 3-year old girl. *International Journal of Psycho-Analysis* 72(1):107–116.

Sussman, M. (1992). *A Curious Calling: Unconscious Motivations for Practicing Psychotherapy.* Northvale, NJ: Jason Aronson.

Theodosakis, J., Adderly, B., and Fox, B. (1997). *The Arthritis Cure.* New York: St. Martin's Press.

Tiller, J., Macrae, A., Schmidt, U., et al. (1994). The prevalence of eating disorders in thyroid disease: a pilot study. *Journal of Psychosomatic Research* 38(6):609–616.

Tschuschke, V., and Dies, R. R. (1994). Intensive analysis of therapeutic factors and outcome in long-term inpatient groups. *International Journal of Group Psychotherapy* 44(2): 185–207.

Tyler, V. (1994). *Herbs of Choice. The Therapeutic Use of Phytomedicines.* New York: Pharmaceutical Products Press.

University of California at Berkeley Wellness Encyclopedia (1995). New York: Houghton Mifflin Company.

University of California at Berkeley Wellness Letter (1996a). DHEA—the promise of youth and health 12/4: January 1–2.

——— (1996b). Beta carotene pills: Should you take them? 12/7: April 1–2.

——— (1996c). Make "folacin" a household word 12/8: May 1–2.

——— (1996d). Garlic: great for cooking, but not much else 12/9: June 1–2.

——— (1996e). Don't let the salt news shake you up 12/12: September 1–2.

——— (1996f). Can you count on Co Q-10? 13/1: October: 2.

————— (1997). Can pond scum really keep you healthy? 13/4: January 1–2.

Vaillant, G. E. (1983). *The Natural History of Alcoholism: Causes, Patterns and Paths to Recovery.* Cambridge, MA: Harvard University Press.

van der Kolk, B. A. (1987). *Psychological Trauma.* Washington, DC: American Psychiatric Press.

Vannicelli, M. (1982). Group psychotherapy aftercare for alcoholic patients. *International Journal of Group Psychotherapy* 38(33):337–353.

Vannicelli, M., Canning, D., and Griefen, M. (1984). Group therapy with alcoholics: a group case. *International Journal of Group Psychotherapy* 34:127–147.

Vivona, J., Ecker, B., Halgin, R., et al. (1995). Self- and other-directed aggression in child and adolescent psychiatric inpatients. *Journal of the American Academy of Child and Adolescent Psychiatry* 34(4):434–444.

Volmar, F. R., Bacon, S., Shakir, S. A., and Pfefferbaum, A. (1981). Group therapy in the management of manic-depressive illness. *American Journal of Psychotherapy* 35: 226–234.

Walker, M. (1994). DHEA: the mother of all hormones. *Nutritional Medicine*, October, pp. 7–10.

Wallach, J. (1996). *Dead Doctors Don't Lie.* Audiotape. Distributed by Norton's Nutrition (800-432-5888).

Waller, G. (1993). Association of sexual abuse and borderline personality disorder in eating disordered women. *International Journal of Eating Disorders* 13(3):259–263.

Wallis, C. (1996). Faith and healing. *Time*, June 24, pp. 58–70.

Ward, B. (1995). Holistic medicine. *Australian Family Physician*, May, pp. 761–765.

Washton, A., and Boundy, D. (1989). *Willpower Is Not Enough: Recovering from Addictions of Every Kind.* New York: HarperCollins.

Weil, A. (1995). *Spontaneous Healing.* New York: Knopf.

——— (1996a). Ask Dr. Weil. *Natural Health Magazine*, August, p. 22.

——— (1996b). Blue-green algae: a cautionary note. *Self Healing*, December: p. 6.

——— (1997). Colloidal minerals: more hype than help. *Self Healing*, March: p. 8.

Wexler, B. E., Johnson, D., Gelles, J., and Gordon, J. (1984). Group psychotherapy with schizophrenic patients: an example of the oneness group. *International Journal of Group Psychotherapy* 34:451–471.

White, M. T., and Weiner, M. B. (1986). *The Theory and Practice of Self Psychology.* New York: Brunner/Mazel.

Wild, R., ed. (1994). *Natural and Medicinal Cures.* Emmaus, PA: Rodale Press.

Williams, P. (1996). Tight fitting genes. *Runners World*, June, p. 19.

Wong, N. (1980). Focus issues in group psychotherapy of borderline narcissistic patients. In *Group and Family Therapy*, ed. L. R. Wolberg and M. L. Aronson. New York: Brunner/ Mazel.

Worner, T. M., Zeller, B., Schwartz, H., et al. (1992). Acupuncture fails to improve outcome in alcoholics. *Drug and Alcohol Dependence* 30(2):169–173.

Yalom, I. D. (1974). Group therapy and alcoholics. *Annals of New York Academy of Science* 233:85–103.

———— (1975). *The Theory and Practice of Group Psychotherapy*, 2nd ed. New York: Basic Books.

York, J. L., and Hirsch, J. A. (1995). Drinking patterns and health status in smoking and nonsmoking alcoholics. *Alcoholism, Clinical and Experimental Research* 19(3):666–673.

Zaidi, L.Y. (1994). Group treatment of adult male inpatients abused as children. *Journal of Traumatic Stress* 7(4):718–727.

Zerhusen, J. D., Boyle, K., and Wilson, W. (1991). Out of the darkness: group cognitive therapy for the depressed elderly. *Journal of Psychosocial Nursing and Mental Health Services* 29(9):16–21.

Zhdanova, I., and Wurtman, R. (1996). How does melatonin affect sleep? *The Harvard Mental Health Letter*, June, p. 8.

Zigmund, V. (1995). Problems with the limitations of medicine. *Bratislavske Lekarske Listy* (Slovak), February, pp. 63–68.

Index